JEAN-PAUL SARTRE

LIVES ON

BEN WOOD JOHNSON

EDUKA SOLUTIONS
Middletown, PA

Life is now; there is no life-after-life. Enjoy your life in the present. Don't waste your precious time today hoping for a better tomorrow.—BWJ/2017

EDUKA SOLUTIONS

Sartre Lives On, by Ben Wood Johnson

This book was first published in 2017

Eduka Solutions
330 W. Main St #214
Middletown, PA, 17057, USA

Printed in the United States of America

Johnson, Ben Wood
    Sartre Lives On /
    Ben Wood Johnson.
    Includes bibliographical references and index.

ISBN-13: 978-0-9979028-4-6 (Paperback)
ISBN-10: 0-9979028-4-1

Available in both print and eBook formats

Cover illustration by Wood Oliver J

TABLE OF CONTENTS

PREFACE

The first edition of the book titled *Sartre Lives On* was originally published in 2017. It was not in an unblemished state. In response to feedback and comments, it became necessary to amend the text, which occurred frequently. I made stylistic and grammatical corrections as I discovered them. Over the years, I noticed several issues that prompted a complete overhaul of the manuscript.

This edition is exploratory; it does not make any ontological assertions about Jean-Paul Sartre or his many publications about human ontology. While this book offers a defense of Jean-Paul Sartre, the arguments presented here do not rebuff, though not thoroughly, popular views against the man or his philosophy. Despite its limits, the text fills an important gap in the literature. The arguments noted here are captivating, while refuting misguided notions with an honest tone.

The writing is succinct. It includes five sections; they are concise. The first section introduces the topic. The second section explores Sartre's literary reach. It relates the context of his role in the literature. The third section examines the nature of criticisms of Sartre. It echoes a need to explore the basis of existing disagreements. The section relates why Sartre is despised in most intellectual corners.

The fourth section contrasts the Sartrean approach to various issues with his views about morality. The section explores whether Sartre deserves a place in the ethical discipline. The fifth section discusses my epistemological relevance in compiling this book.

Completing this work was a delight; it was also a daunting experience. Despite the efforts interjected in this softcover, it may not defend Sartre as I had hoped. So long as this tome offers a different side of Jean-Paul Sartre, it would have been worthwhile.

If you would like to learn more about Sartre, you may read this folio from cover to cover. If you would like to learn more about the claims often echoed against Sartre, please see other works on the subject.[1] If you would like to know more about me or my philosophy, see my other works. Some of these publications are listed toward the end of the manuscript. Join me in this discussion.

Good reading!

---

1. I compiled two books about Sartrean ethics. The first one is titled *Sartrean Ethics: A Defense of Jean-Paul Sartre as a Moral Philosopher* (2016) and the second is *Jean-Paul Sartre and Morality: A Legacy Under Attack* (2017). They are available in both paperback and electronic versions.

ACKNOWLEDGMENTS

It is important to take the time to thank the people who influenced this edition. These individuals made up a positive force in my scholastic endeavors. They changed my reasoning around the time my maturity was strong enough to help me make sense of the world around me.

Let me thank Maître Jiko and my dear colleague Saint-Juste for their encouragement. Their thoughtful words and their counsel encouraged me to keep my eyes on the prize, despite the tumults that consumed my life in the summer of 2015. Their words of hope and their compassion helped me face the tsunami of hatred that almost drag my family to the ground.

It is vital to recognize the people whose efforts speeded up this work directly or indirectly. Let me use this moment to thank those who gave me feedback and helpful comments on the final draft. They helped make this intellectual journey a pleasant experience.

Special thanks to Derronette, Collin, Dupui, and my editors (Wolden and Xaon). They read several drafts to help me fine-tune my arguments. They made it possible for me to make the manuscript as perfect as it could be. Their insights helped me find the right tone to convey my views as coherently as possible in Sartre's defense.

It is proper to thank my dear friend Whisler Jean for accepting to proofread the finished manuscript. His contribution is unique to this project. Let me recognize his support publicly.

Thank you!

December 2022
Ben Wood Johnson, Ph.D.

INTRODUCTION

Jean-Paul Sartre was a great intellectual. I have nothing but admiration for the man. For his talents and the quality of his craft, my affinity for Sartre could be described as pure devotion.

Sartre's writings are a source of fascination for me. Sartre himself is a source of inspiration, which allowed to construct my own philosophical brand. However, my interest in Sartre is principally academic. That like-mindedness has more to do with his work about human ontology than anything else.

After reading Sartre's reviews discoursing his positions on human ontology, the idea of freedom has traversed my mind in ways that may seem unusual to most people.[1] Delving in Sartre's works helped me discover the intricacies, which are entrenched in his philosophical paradigm. The Sartrean model to assess human existence informed my own viewpoints. Evaluating the roots of human freedom is at the center of my philosophy. With this confession out of the way, note that it would take more than admirations to consider myself an avid follower of the Sartrean philosophical paradigm, though I describe myself as a devotee of Sartrean philosophy.

---

[1] The book is aptly titled *Being and Nothingness*.

There is enough hostility towards the man. It's hard to find works that are not critical of Sartre. In his defense, these criticisms are in error. There is a need to defend the Sartrean legacy. This collection is an attempt to do just that.

While some observers might question my aptitude for this task, note that my analysis is not inconsequential. My academic foundation may lend me some credence. Evaluating Sartre's philosophical domain is not a new endeavor for me. Such opportunities came up before. I had a similar experience while in high school. During that time, I learned about Sartrean philosophy. In college, I had the chance to conduct inquiries about Sartre. In graduate school, I continued learning about Sartre. Discussing his works in class was a common affair. Examining Sartre's popular treatises was a regular activity in graduate school. As an author, I compiled several works about Sartre. Thus, compiling a defense on Sartre's behalf is merely incidental.

This work lingers on the intellectual path that Sartre was a great philosopher. He played a substantial role in ethics. My literary repertoire includes a few monographs detailing my concerns *vis-à-vis* the state of the present discourse toward Sartre. The book is an addendum to the mentioned works.

The present compilation presents another side of the debate. It features Jean-Paul Sartre under a more positive light, chiefly when it comes to his approach to ethics. The book is informative. It is a well-conceived analysis of Sartre's work. The text may fulfill your curiosity about Sartre.

1. SETTING THE STAGE

Despite my esteem for Jean-Paul Sartre, not to mention my astonishment at his literary accomplishments, a few of the positions Sartre echoed in his works do not sit well with me. There is much to be desired with the Sartrean examination of the reality of human existence in a world designed to do away with that existence. For instance, a Sartrean approach to a person's ability to navigate his world is his responsibility.

The Sartrean model suggests that a man's worth is relevant only based on how he is made out to be in the world that others concocted on his behalf, and not necessarily for his own sake. For Sartre, the man oversees his reality; he oversees his destiny despite the circumstances. He might be forced to fend off in his quotidian with his bare hands and by relying on his derisory thinking abilities to survive on his own and for his own sake. That view could not be further from the truth, though my assertion here may not be in unanimity.

Sartre's work is a brilliant account of the human condition (Sartre and Richmond 2022). He unwittingly denies the realities that underpin human existence in a social milieu. Sartre does not recognize the preponderance of social forms and structures which guide the extent of human existence (Levin 1968). As a rebuttal, Sartre might reference the notion of dialectical reason as a convenient explanation to assign a specific actuality to the man in terms of his assessment of his own *de facto* reality (Levi-strauss 1966).

There is enough reason to disagree with Sartre's depiction of human freedom. There is much envious of Sartre's assessment of human ontology. Notwithstanding my divergences with Sartre about his philosophical model, my esteem for Jean-Paul Sartre is profound.

Sartre is a major thinker. His imprint in human history is permanent. However, critics may disagree with the role Sartre played in philosophy.

WORKS ABOUT JEAN-PAUL SARTRE

Over the last few years, several works about Sartre entered the literary stream. They have assessed the role that Sartre [seemingly] played in ethics. The verdict is unanimous. Most observers believe that Sartre has no place in moral philosophy. But I beg to differ in the present context.

It is irrefutable that Jean-Paul Sartre is among the most famous philosophers in the twentieth century (Sartre 2002; Ledgerwood 1990). He is the principal founder of the movement known as existentialism (Sartre 2002). Sartre is an unparalleled political thinker (Sartre 2002). Yet, views diverge about the man's true intellectual worth.

Some observers dismiss Sartre as a nineteenth-century thinker (Sartre 2001). He is among the most controversial philosophers in history (Ledgerwood 1990). Sartre is also among the most misunderstood thinkers in modern times (Ledgerwood 1990).

The dispute over Sartre's works is not limited to ethics. There is a hesitancy to see Sartre as an influential thinker. Lévi-Strauss, for instance, echoed the charge of ethnocentrism against Sartre for defining the men in dialectical terms (Sartre 2001). Other observers are likely to undermine Sartre based on their little understanding of his works.

Many of the people who lambaste Sartre have little knowledge of his work (Ledgerwood 1990). Some observers simply rely on opinions echoed by other critics to undervalue Sartre's work (Ledgerwood 1990; Poellner 2016). Misreading about Sartre's work results from unrecognized and under-interpreted accounts. It is also because of ambiguities in Sartre's own utterances (Poellner 2016). It might be hard to share the view that the work of Sartre produced is inconsequential or irrelevant.

The Sartrean legacy lives on. He has remained the most important French thinker of the twentieth century (Ledgerwood 1990). He will probably remain that way for years to come (Ledgerwood 1990). There is an enduring interest in Sartre himself (Arthur 2007). But that interest is not always for his benefits.

Most works about Sartrean philosophy are about Sartre himself. Such works point out flaws in the works Sartre produced. Similar failings, many are convinced, show Sartre's literary valor. There is a need to debunk that view.

DEFENDING SARTRE

It is central to survey whether Sartre was respected as a writer while alive and even postmortem. There is a need to consider the nature of Sartre's literary repertoire. This work notes the extent to which Sartre's work, chiefly posthumously released materials, is rightfully contended.

Discussing Sartre's ethics is difficult. It is not simple to dissect the writings of a brilliant thinker. There might be questions about the relevance of this work, considering there is no dearth of information about Sartre. Nonetheless, the views echoed here are unique.

Why is there a need to defend Sartre? Does this edition reveal anything novel in the debate? The answer to the former question is clear. The Sartrean legacy is under attack. However, the answer to the latter question might be hard to determine, although the analysis presented in this context might apply to the current debate over the role Sartre might have played in moral philosophy.

The present edition does not cover the latest information on Sartre. It does not explore the man in depth. It does not examine his works further than exploring ideas that already exist in the literature. However, this collection sketches out the philosophy of Jean-Paul Sartre distinctly.

The title offers a candid recount of Sartre's story. It centers on the man and his legacy. The text frames the debate positively. It is a clever way of presenting Sartre.

While the idea of defending Sartre may sound pompous, its relevance can be undeniable. Certainly, only Sartre can defend his intellectual repertoire. Only he can protect his own legacy. This work could not substitute Sartre's view of his own accomplishments.

This composition is concise. Sartre was an important thinker. Although his philosophical approach may not be perfect, there needs to be a balance in the debate. The conversation is never in Sartre's favor. This manual tries to correct that.

ARGUMENTATIVE LIMITS

This volume, brief though it is, debates the Sartrean signature on ontology. It does not address the crux of ideals Sartre echoed about human existence. The text assesses the extent to which Sartrean ethics is based on the works that Sartre produced while alive or released posthumously.

The book examines the Sartrean approach to morality. However, it does so by exploring how Sartre understood the person (that is, the being). The text explores the issues based on how Sartre thought the person should see the self in the world.

As we move along in this composition, a few limits are worthy of note. First, the document does not debate the details of Sartrean ethics. Other works are more explanatory on the topic. Second, the text does not discuss every quarrel that is often levied against Sartre. Third, the document does not revisit the intricacies of the Sartrean ethical model.

The book is not the product of a rigorous inquiry. It is not empirical. It is broad in scope, though the aim is to discuss the issues as succinctly as possible. The tome relays my genuine concerns over the scorn that prevails in the debate against Sartre. The views expressed here are valid, though biased, considering I have a bias in the debate.

Reading this paperback is not a fruitless pursuit. The views outlined in it are informative. There is a need to intimate a meticulous examination of the current debate.

As outlined earlier, the book is not exhaustive. This is merely an introductory sample other works, which are more thorough about the Sartrean philosophical imprint. To that extent, the book does not delve in the matters that constitute the literature over the role Jean-Paul Sartre played in moral philosophy or elsewhere.[1] In any case, this is a carefully designed collection of ideas debunking falsehoods about the man, his philosophy, and his accomplishments.

---

[1] See the text Sartre Ethics to learn more about the Sartrean approach to moral philosophy.

Let us delve a little deeper into the debate. Let us ponder on why Jean-Paul Sartre was so eerily despised. Let us discuss what will happen to his legacy. It is important to decipher potential ways to salvage Sartre's reputation both as a brilliant thinker and a prolific writer.

SECTION ONE

Introducing Jean-Paul Sartre

2. Sartre and His Critics

Who was Jean-Paul Sartre? This question recurs in later chapters. Here, we could say that Sartre was a famous thinker. Most people would say that Sartre was a brilliant theorist. Sartre was a philosopher like no other. Yet, this view is not in unanimity.

Observers often justify their criticisms of Sartre by referencing the same texts and actions, which premise, it could be said, Sartre designed to echo a specific point of view supporting his communist ideals during the 1950s (Arthur 2007, 231). Critics conflate these ideas intentionally. They offer them as proof that Sartre's literary valor should be diminished in consequence.

There are many points of strife against Sartre in the literature. Most people have a love-hate relationship with the man. Since the 1940s, Sartre has always been criticized both from the left and from the right of the ideological spectrum (Birchall 2004). Even the feminist interpretations of Sartre's work have left much to be desired. For instance, in most feminist corners, the pervading belief is that Sartrean philosophy is male oriented (Murphy 1999). That philosophy, Murphy (1999) notes, is useless to women.

Sartre is also criticized in his explicit theoretical ideas (LaCapra 2019). With his approach to existentialism, notably the Marxist understandings, Sartre's theory is not impervious to criticism (Flynn 1986). However, while some people are likely to challenge Sartre as an intellectual, others are likely to rebuff him as a person. Emerick (1999) notes an avid desire by Sartre's critics to misinterpret his ideas. They also misrepresent such ideas (Emerick 1999). It is a reality Emerick describes as a deliberate commission of a straw man fallacy (Emerick 1999). This approach to Sartre's work is misguided.

Critics often reproduce obsessively cold war rhetoric about Sartre and his works to obscure the man and his philosophical accomplishments (Arthur 2007, 231). Critics are likely to ignore Sartre's great political engagement on various fronts, including his participation in the national liberation and anticolonialism resistance movements around the world (Arthur 2007, 231). It is as if to suggest that Sartre had no relevance to popular culture and politics (Arthur 2007, 231).

SARTRE HAS NO MORAL CHARACTER

The pervading belief is that Sartre was not the best moral character. While this work does not detail this facet of the debate, there is a need to revisit facets of these arguments in greater length to clarify the notion that Sartre was despised both publicly and privately. There is a need to move past the tendency to look at Sartre from a *cold war* lens, which does little to no justice to his views, chiefly on political violence (Arthur 2007, 231). Criticisms against Sartre are unbound.

In human history, a lot has been said about Sartre; a lot has been written, either in academic circles or elsewhere, about Sartre's ideas, his views, or his works. It may be impossible to save Sartre's personal reputation. We could still salvage his literary legacy. Despite it all, Sartre continues to live on. His place in modern literature is irrefutable. This collection of short essays echoes that reality as soundly as possible. Thus, this edition is an insightful realignment of the current debate about Sartre.

Sartre was a controversial figure during his time. To this day, his philosophical bearing is still contested. My intent is to examine the literary tentacles of this great thinker and philosopher as succinctly as possible. Granted, I could only do so from a particular angle.

The hope in compiling this book is to present a coherent defense on Sartre's behalf. That defense shall be is succinct, for it will not relay every facet of Sartrean philosophy. Instead, the focus of my analysis is on Sartrean ethics.

This work offers a different perspective on the debate. For one, it outlines a simpler framework for understanding the foundation of Sartrean philosophy. Second, it helped the reader make sense of the role that Sartre played in ethics. Sartre contributes to the ethical discipline by linking his views about human ontology with his ethical ideas. Sartre imagined ethics as an important side of human conduct tied up with human existence.

A DEPRESSING REALITY

The literature about Sartrean philosophy can be revolting and even depressing. Jean-Paul Sartre is often attacked because (they say) he did not outline his ideas soundly. His philosophy, critics often denote, justifies revolutionary violence and terror (Arthur 2007, 231). this assessment of Sartre's works is subjective; it is misguided; it is biased at its core. Sartre is often scolded for not putting his ideas in a universally accepted way.

A side of the philosophy of Jean-Paul Sartre is laden with criticisms. For example, most observers do not think that Sartre is a moral philosopher. They challenge his works on ethics. For most observers, the Sartrean approach to ethics is miserly; if not, it is intellectually inconsequential. Sartre's works in this discipline, many are convinced, are vague. Else, they are incomplete.

The literature has many overzealous assessments of the works Sartre produced throughout his career. These views are based on mistaken beliefs about the man, his thinking, or his contribution to ethics. Sartre is accused of many offenses, including that of being an anti-European thinker (Mcdonnell 2020). That view is misguided, for it does not consider the fact that Sartre saw Europe as an ongoing project and not as a place with a static identity (Mcdonnell 2020). Despite the many claims often echoed against Sartre, his role in human literature is fixed and can be undeniable.

Many people believe that Sartre is not a moral philosopher. It is that way under any circumstances. Emerick (1999) disagrees with the notion that Sartre's theory can lose their intellectual values because of criticisms. The degree to which criticisms against Sartre undermines his work remains a highly contested debate.

Sartre's philosophical development is above that of his literary criticism (Suhl 1999). The usual claim against Sartre is that he is archaic (Cooper 1964). Such a survey of Sartre's literary valor is not in unanimity; at least, it is hard for me to see Sartre with a similar lens. This work echoes that disagreement clearly.

It is important to dissect the congruity of Sartre's literary portfolio. The goal is to decipher the man, his views, his passion, and his contributions to literature. Sartre was among thinkers like Maurice Merleau-Ponty and Emmanuel Levinas, contributed to spreading the notion of phenomenology in France (Raynova 2002) and subsequently around the world. Sartre's single-handedly changed salient facets of ideas Husserl echoed in his takes on the phenomenology of existence, which is characterized by the living experience (Raynova 2002). Another goal of this analysis, which is stated more implicitly, is to explore Sartre's past in the most fitting way.

We ought to examine the ideas Sartre made popular during his career. It is important to study views criticizing Sartre's ethics. It is urgent to relate criticisms against Sartre as an intellectual artisan.

A CONCILIATORY APPROACH

This edition is undersized, compared to other publications debating the subject. While the manuscript is not extensive, it is part of a collection of essays about Sartre, which I completed years ago. These works are extracts from a research paper, which I compiled while in graduate school.

Even though this edition is not original (per se), it is academically relevant. It relates the issues from a much wider angle as opposed to the previously mentioned works. It offered the reader a broader, but also a succinct, understanding of the issues that pervade the literature about Sartrean philosophy.

There is an awareness of a conciliatory approach in the current dialogue on Sartre's literate valor. Paige Arthur echoed that need in his piece, advocating for a better treatment of Sartre's views, which criticism from Arthur's vantage point is based on a flawed assumption about the man and his literary valor. Arthur (2007) notes that critics ignore other works Sartre produce throughout his career and focus on his assessment of decolonization, as prefaced in Frantz Fanon's text, *The Wretched of the Earth*, as evidence that Sartre had missed the mark on these issues (Arthur 2007, 231). Sartre's literary contribution to Fanon's opus does not resume the positions he took elsewhere, notably in more sustained works, including *The Critique of Dialectical Reason* and his *Role Lecture* on ethics (in 1964) (Arthur 2007, 231). There is a need to re-evaluate existing disagreements about Jean-Paul Sartre. We ought to assess his most striking writings. It is a duty to defend this unparalleled thinker, which I take seriously in this book and elsewhere.

Despite the contentious nature of the debate, this tome is not an unproductive tirade about Sartre or against his most enthusiastic critics. Instead, the paperback proposes a more jovial examination of the works that Sartre produced and released to the public, both during his career and after he passed away.

3. A Philosophical Brilliance

Voltaire put it so eloquently: *Le génie n'a qu'un siècle, après quoi, il faut qu'il se dégénère* (CCM Benchmark 2022) That is, the reign of a genie could only last one century. Any literal lecture of this quote suggests that a person who has genie-like qualities could only influence his or her environment for a limited time, preferably for one century.

This popular adage is based on ideals that have remained undisputed for many centuries. It might be difficult to question its accuracy. It might be impossible to undermine the intellectual potency of this viewpoint. From this understanding, every genie has one century to be relevant in his or her sphere of expertise. The idea is to describe the previously noted approach as the "one century per genie" paradigm.

Sartre was a genius in his own right. He dominated his intellectual era unprecedentedly. He was considered a reigning intellectual (Flynn 2005). Sartre understood his responsibilities as a writer for his time. In his writings, Sartre notes that the writer has an engagement toward his audience (Martinot 1999). A writer must situate the self as he writes in and for his time (Martinot 1999). The writer takes part in the historical moment in which he lives. Unlike most geniuses in the history of humankind, Sartre's time seems infinite, though Flynn (2000) notes that the Sartrean time is progressive at its core. Sartre's time is also moral (Flynn 2000).

From most people's vantage point, Sartre is a relevant philosopher. As an author, Sartre is regarded as an unparalleled writer. As a thinker, observers consider him a genie in his own right. Yet, the belief that Sartre was a great intellectual is often contested (passionately) in certain literary corners.

Distinctly, the thinking is that Sartre played little or no role in human literature. He played no relevant role in ethics, they say. It might be hard to share this argument. A noteworthy aim is to discredit similar views throughout this text. Sartrean ethics exist, though most observers would say otherwise.[1] In this context, doing the same is reasonable.

THE CALIBER OF JEAN-PAUL SARTRE

There are those who believe that Sartre is the greatest theorist whose intellectual tentacles within the social world have extended farther than those of Sigmund Freud.[2] His philosophical thoughts, many have argued, continue to dominate the literary conversation. For an array of observers, the quality of Sartre's works, including the diverse nature of the writings, which Sartre put together can be irrefutable.[3] For many admirers of Jean-Paul Sartre, the influence of the works which, he produced, both while alive and posthumously, extends over half a century.[4] Sartre has a significant influence

---

1. See my other publication about Sartrean ethics, including (Johnson 2016) to learn more about Jean-Paul Sartre and his views about moral philosophy.

[2] To learn more about this idea, see (Johnson 2016)

[3] To learn more about this idea, see (Johnson 2016)

[4] You can learn more about this idea. Please, see (Johnson 2016)

in philosophy, literature, politics, and cultural studies (Sartre 2002).

It is undisputable that Jean-Paul Sartre did a lot during his lifetime. He was a successful philosopher; he was a brilliant writer. Sartre knew how to bend the words; he knew how to set up his arguments to suggest the message that he looked to share with his audience. Sartre was an unsurpassed illustrator.

There is no need to debate the nature of Sartre's philosophical competence at length. It might be difficult, if not impossible, to deny that Sartre did a lot during his lifetime. Without a doubt, Sartre was a successful philosopher. He was a brilliant writer.

Sartre knew how to use his words to have an impact. He knew how to frame his arguments in a way that carries the message he wanted to share with his audience. There is no deliberation about that fact; Sartre was an unrivaled intellectual choreographer. He was a literary genius.

Sartre knew how to capture our minds; he knew how to play with our imagination. Sartre was the psychoanalyst; he could read us telepathically.

Sartre knew how to captivate our intellectual curiosity. As a thinker, Sartre never asked us to reveal ourselves to him before he could undress our reality in the most intimate way. Sartre was the expert in his own art.

Sartre was the intellectual equivalent of a priest, a Voodoo Priest, some might say. The earlier viewpoint is not echoed with contempt. In some cultures, a voodoo cleric is presumed to be someone who could see reality, which most people could not see or even understand with the naked eyes. Such a person has direct access to a world that is omnipresent, but still obscure to most minds or eyes. Sartre, one could argue, had such a faculty.

Sartre was indeed the intellectual equivalent of a voodoo cleric. But as a truth seeker, Sartre had such a competence only if one were to examine the man from an unbiased prism or with an unfiltered mindset. The same could be said if we were to examine Sartre through an intellectual lens.

Sartre was in contact with a dimension of the world which few of us could recognize, at least not on our own. In the philosophical realm, Sartre was the link between the real and the surreal. He seemed in charge of his reality. Sartre was on top of the world in which we live.

The earlier contentions are rare. If they existed at all, they would be ignored. The debate does not consider Sartre as a worthy intellectual. Viewpoints supporting the notion that Sartre might be a moral philosopher are artlessly rebuked. From here, the Sartrean contribution to human literature is caricatured in a not so flattery manner. The consensus is that Sartre was a failure. Is there any truth to this viewpoint? The answer is no. Granted, there is a need to prove that assertion beyond any doubt.

SARTRE AND ETHICAL WRITINGS

Despite Jean-Paul Sartre's accomplishments, questions are still about Sartre's intellectual success in many fields, chiefly in the ethical genre. Some observers refuse to recognize Sartre's intellectual brilliance in ethics. Critics often question the nature of Sartre's skill in this domain.

Other observers have debated, with scorn, the nature of Sartre's philosophical application in ethics. The pervading belief among many critics is that Sartre was not that prolific as a philosopher. His intellectual competence was exaggerated, they say. But I see Sartre differently.

Sartre played a substantive role in the human literature. His contribution to moral philosophy is only secondary to those of prominent thinkers, such as René Descartes, Jean-Jacques Rousseau, Karl Marx, Immanuel Kant, and Friedrich Nietzsche, among others. Even Sartre's take on existentialism is an amalgam of ideas extracted from popular thinkers, including, but not limited to, Husserl, Marx, Heidegger, and Nietzsche. Despite that plausibility, Sartre was also an influential thinker. Although most critics would agree with that statement, others would deny the idea that Sartre left a permanent mark in moral philosophy. These observers are confused about Sartre. The man was an accomplished thinker in ethics. This is clear in the many works Sartre produced during his career, even the works released on his behalf postmortem.

Although most people might disagree with Sartre's positions on certain issues, be they social, political, or else, that does not lessen the intellectual relevance of such issues, nor should it be the case that such a disagreement ineluctably makes Sartre's take on these societal problems inconsequential. Despite arguments claiming the contrary, Sartre was not an enigma in literature. He was not an obscure thinker. Sartre was well read. His intellectual repertoire is well known and extremely appreciated.

Considering the works that Sartre produced, he was an influential thinker. That does not mean his works were perfect. There are disagreements on the quality of the literary materials Sartre produced over the years. Most observers disagree with Sartre's views on certain philosophical principles. While many of these views have merit, others are more spiteful toward the man and his craft than anything else. Thus, they have no intellectual relevance, which is worthy of note.

The most contentious criticism against Sartre is for his works about ethics. It would not make sense to deny Sartre his intellectual dues simply because we disagree with his views on certain notions. Sartre deserves his well-earned literary notoriety.

A PHILOSOPHICAL PIONEER

Most people are not avid Sartre readers. Few people would agree that Sartre contributed to popular culture, both while alive and posthumously, lavishly. There is a need to relate that understanding as coherently as possible.

Before we go further, note this work is not the result of an empirical investigation. In the start, it is worthy of note that my potential biased view could be a rightful concern. Thus, you might take my arguments with skepticism.

Yes, the present title does not offer a neutral examination of the current literary conversation. But that does not (or should not) undermine its literary relevance. As noted earlier, I enjoy reading Sartre's works. To reiterate an earlier concession, I have a biased viewpoint, which will become bare as you navigate the text.

It is incontrovertible that Sartre was a pioneer in philosophical writings. The Sartrean literary imprint is permanent. His works extend in several genres. Sartre wrote about philosophy. He drafted a few provocative books in other fields and disciplines. Sartre also produced plays; he produced novels. He compiled works about theater, biography, psychology, and politics (Aronson and Hoven 1991, 26). The Sartrean literary reach is extensive.

Sartre is among the most studied thinkers in human history. Toward the end of the 1950s, the man was criticized for his positions against the West, while denying the

Communist Party (Aronson and Hoven 1991, 24). Sartre became the most despised man in France (Aronson and Hoven 1991, 24). Even after his death, Sartre is still despised in most circles. What might explain that?

I do not offer a forthright answer, which might help clarify why Sartre is criticized so much. One may lack clarity about the reason his works are often lessened or even rebuffed. It may not be obvious to the uninformed observers about why most people have a dislike for the man. What seems certain is that Sartre is hated. Contempt toward the Sartrean literary trademark can be visceral and even virulent.

It became impossible to clarify the reason Sartre was despised both as a person and as a thinker. I did not live through the era that saw him mature both personally and intellectually. I did not experience what Sartre went through in life. I did not know Sartre more than anyone else did. It might be futile to pretend to be the bearer of truth about Jean-Paul Sartre.

While my knowledge of Sartrean philosophy is genuine, it is based on what I have had the chance to read about the man in the literature. The views that underpinned this rebuttal are based on what others have said about his works, though it was important to consider existing claims from an idealistic mindset.

Sartre's works result from my astuteness of Sartre's intent after reading his famous publications, chiefly the works he produced on ethics. Sartre contributed lavishly to this discipline. Assessing criticisms against Sartre was based chiefly on ideas that became clear to me while glancing at Sartre's literary accomplishments. It was conceivable to evaluate his works directly or by assessing the views others echoed in their writings after engaging in similar assessments of the same works.

4. COMPLETE BEWILDERMENT

Commentators often ask about the reason Jean-Paul Sartre has remained such a prominent figure in the literature. Others have wondered why the Sartrean intellectual legacy is consequential so many years after his death. Observers have asked about the reason (or reasons) Sartre's works kept their popularity for so long. No one has the answer.

In recent years, several inquirers have asked the earlier questions frequently and relentlessly. Although they did so in different settings, their efforts have been futile. Other tries to unravel the nature of Sartrean ethics have been to no use.

Few people have been able to offer substantive answers on whether Sartrean Ethics exists. Until now, the extent of Sartrean philosophy left many observers perplexed. Sartre is still a mystery, even to his peers.

Sartre defies the one-century-by-genie model, which is echoed in the beginning of the text.[1] Sartre has had a similar impact in several disciplines. His works continue to resound in various circles. His plays continue to be relatable; they are even popular in the theatrical genre.

Sartre's contribution to the literature is relevant in several ways. His imprints, for instance, are lasting in the present-day

---

[1] Please refer to the earlier chapter to make sense of the notion of a one-genie-per-century paradigm.

literature. Many scholars and ordinary observers alike are amused by the reason this is the case. It is undeniable that Sartre developed a new lens, which allowed him to examine the singularity of the person in the environment where he lives.

Commentators, mostly critics, bloggers, and casual readers of French literature or classical philosophy, poignantly wonder about the reason (or reasons) so many people are fascinated with Sartre. Well-known scholars have also conducted extensive surveys about the reason Sartre's views on several topics, namely his approach to morality, have incited so many debates, which are often enthusiastic.

I am curious about the reason critics have sought to decipher the ambit of Sartrean philosophy. There are questions about Sartre. The literature seems overwhelmed with disputes against Sartre. There is no need to address these issues in depth here. It is that way for distinct reasons. Many of the questions levied against Sartre are unanswered or are answered with a biased view. There is no need to belabor the point. This is not the purpose of this essay. Let us explore a few of these questions here.

UNANSWERED QUESTIONS

There are so many questions about Jean-Paul Sartre that he should have been regarded as a well-known thinker by now. There have been so many investigations of his work that a lack of answers about Sartre's thoughts on certain precepts is baffling. Existing questions about Sartre could be valid if they are answered properly. Such answers would help us understand the extent of Sartre's thought process.

In many respects, fewer inquiries (including scholarly investigations) have been able to offer objective answers or any practical explanations of Sartre. They could not clarify the essence of Sartre's main ideas. Sartrean philosophy is still a mystery to many people. For most observers, Sartre is an enigma both as a writer and a philosopher.

Despite Sartre's popularity, he is an unknown philosopher. What could explain this phenomenon? One may become lost in the debate about how to approach this question. Few critics could offer satisfactory answers.

There is a lack of positive perspectives about Sartre. One reason to consider this is that people are quick to rebuff Sartre's views on certain issues. Some are quick to disagree with Sartre's work in various fields, including moral philosophy. They do so vocally. This might explain the reason Sartrean philosophy is inscrutable in various literary circles.

Few observers seem interested in lauding Sartre. Over the years, several commentators have become common to criticize Sartre unabashedly. There is a relentless pursuit to depict Sartre as a lesser thinker than he was.

It seems easier to point out flaws in Sartre's works. There is no fervor to give Sartre credit for his work. Few people would accept Sartre's achievements genuinely. Many of Sartre's fervent critics come from diverse levels of society. They include bloggers, scholars, commentators, literary critics, and pundits, to name a few. Sartre is often smeared ferociously on many fronts.

Sartre's works are rebuffed unrepentantly. There is a tendency to rebuke Sartre with no serious considerations. This reality could explain why Sartre is often the subject of endless investigations.

A CONSPIRACY APPROACH

Is there a conspiracy against Jean-Paul Sartre? I am not sure how to respond. What is unambiguous is that the man is bitterly despised. Unlike most philosophers in human history, Sartre is not always understood both as a person and as an intellectual. There is much contempt for this thinker. To restate, few commentators would admit Sartre's true contribution to human literature.

Another important side about critics against Sartre is worthy of note. For example, many people have adopted a conspiracy approach to examining criticisms against Sartre. There is the notion that Sartre was slandered because he held views that were not necessarily compatible with popular viewpoints.

There is a complexity in the debate. Sartre was often regarded as a renegade. In some social circles, he was even considered an agitator. Many pundits regarded Sartre as an intellectual vagabond, to put it mildly.

For most Sartrean enthusiasts, there is more to the issues than is otherwise obvious to most observers. Many people are convinced that there is a guided effort to deprive Sartre of his well-earned literary legacy. While there is no need to question this view, agreeing with the idea that Sartre is unfairly treated may not be so difficult.

The reason critics see little or no use for Sartrean philosophy can easily become hard to pinpoint. As noted earlier, Sartre was indeed a prolific writer. He compiled many works about his thinking. Sartre published more than a few writings on morality. Yet, one has the sense that Sartre did little during his literary career. For most observers, Sartre did extraordinarily little in the ethical genre. The question is why people see Sartre that way.

There is a need to be critical of the critics. There is a need to examine the nature of criticisms, many of which of unhinged, against Sartre. We ought to revisit some of Sartre's most famous works. It is important to decipher the nature of the state of bewilderment which pervades the current conversation. It is supreme to shed some light on the issues, which permeate the debate over the degree to which Jean-Paul Sartre was indeed a noteworthy thinker. It is equally necessary to examine the arguments that are often levied to deny Sartre as a moral philosopher.

SARTRE'S LITERARY IMPRINT

Jean-Paul Sartre was a philosopher in the genuine sense of the word. Despite criticisms, or regardless of arguments to the contrary, he was a thinker with incommensurable talents. Thomas Anderson notes that it may be hard for any thinker in the twentieth century to match Sartre in terms of his talents. It would be hard to find a thinker who could rival Sartre in terms of his many talents (Anderson 2002a).

Sartre's talents include playwright, psychologist, novelist, otologist, short story writer, philosophical anthropologist, social and political philosopher and critic, biographer, aesthetician, philosopher of history, and ethicist (Anderson 2002a). As an essayist, Sartre is among the most important moralists of his time (Wreszin 1961). Even some of Sartre's most avid critics recognized his genius in many fields. They are quick to rebuke his work. Some observers say that there is more to the slight for Sartre. Agreeing with that taxation may be harder than most would admit.

It is irrefutable that Sartre has a literary imprint; that intellectual dent is worthy of note. Sartre was a fertile writer. The notion that Sartre was a philosophical misnomer is mistaken. Who was Sartre?

Sartre was born in Paris (France) on June 21, 1905. He died (in France as well) on April 15, 1980. His works have lived on. Sartre lives on in several literary corners.

The Sartrean model had a major impact on popular culture. He influenced other thinkers. His ideas transcended generations. There are no misgivings about this reality; Sartre was a transcendental figure in modern-day literature.

Sartre left his intellectual imprints in several literary genres. During Sartre's lifetime, he produced books, plays, and other items. Between 1936 and 2005, Sartre published over forty-five books, including manuscripts, playwrights, and other publications. Out of these forty-five works, eight of them were posthumous publications, which had been released by his daughter, Arlette Elkaïm-Sartre.[2]

On average, Sartre published one book each year. His most prolific years include 1946, 1947, 1965, and 1983. In each of those years, Sartre published at least three books. By any standard, this achievement was an extraordinary feat. Some might say that this was typical of the Sartrean aura in contemporaneous literature. Sartre was a talented writer; he was an atypical thinker. These traits were obvious in many of his published works.

The next section features many of the works Sartre produced, both while alive and after a postmortem. Note that the items outlined in this work do not come from an exhaustive inquiry. The list is not a correct depiction of every single work which Sartre produced or published during his long literary career. Despite these limits, the information presented in this edition might help clarify the extent of the Sartrean literary imprint in human history.

---

[2] To learn more about this understanding, you may see: (Johnson 2017).

SARTRE'S MAJOR WORKS

Sartre authored novels, plays, short stories, political pamphlets, and philosophical writings. He wrote extensively about phenomenological ontology. Sartre also wrote comprehensively about moral philosophy. These works, as I will echo further, are often labeled incomplete.

Critics are convinced that these works are not suitable for ethics. Then, they could not cement Sartre as a worthy contributor to the genre. Sartre's ethical writings are not comprehensive enough to place him in the ranks of moral philosophers. I will analyze the criticisms in later chapters.

Among the major works Sartre produced, I could mention: Nausea (1938), The Wall (1939), Being and Nothingness (1943), The Age of Reason (1945), Existentialism and Humanism (1946), anti-Semite and Jew (1946), No Exit and Three Other Plays (1947), What is Literature (1948), Critique of Dialectical Reason (1960), The Words (1963), and among other publications.

Sartre was influenced by several major figures in philosophy. Among the people who influenced Sartre includes individuals, such as Raymond Aron, Maurice Merleau-Ponty, Albert Camus, Simone de Beauvoir, Alain Badiou, Michel Foucault, and Frantz Fanon, to name a few.

Sartre was known for several of his works. He was also famous for the words or phrases that he often reflected throughout his writings. In the publication titled *Jean-Paul Sartre and Morality: A Legacy Under Attack*, popular words, phrases, and quotes that Sartre regularly uttered or mentioned during his career became the pièce de résistance, which gave the book a well-deserved point of interest. These entries are available in both French and English. They include:

"L'enfer, c'est les autres." "Hell is for the others/Hell is for other people."

"L'existence précède l'essence." "Existence precedes essence."

"La vie est une passion inutile." "Life is a useless passion."

"La mort est la continuité de ma vie sans moi…" "Death is a continuation of my life without me…"

"Le néant hante étant." "Nothingness haunts being."

"Peut-on juger une vie sur un seul acte ?" "Can we judge a life on a single act?"

The earlier entries are a sample of the brilliant ideas that Sartre echoed in his most famous works. You may refer to the mentioned publications directly; otherwise, you may consult others works to learn more about Sartre. You may discover more about the extent of the Sartrean legacy by finding some of my other works. For instance, you may see the text titled Jean-Paul Sartre: A Legacy Under Attack to learn more about Sartre's most famous words and phrases.[3]

---

3. These quotes are also available on the popular website known as goodreads.com.

SECTION 2

The Sartrean Literary Legacy

5. A PHILOSOPHER PAR EXCELLENCE

Jean-Paul Sartre was a philosopher par excellence. The man spent most of his life in France, contributing to culture and literature. Sartre was also a global voice. He was popular in other countries. His incontestable fame (not to mention his recognition) extended beyond the geographical boundaries of the French Republic, which is known as "L'Hexagone."[1] Sartre was a universal philosopher.

A side of Sartre is rarely recounted in positive terms, principally in recent memory. I am referring to his works in ethics. It is vital to underline the intellectual supremacy of this great thinker in the ethical discipline.

The ideas echoed here note that Sartre was a moral philosopher. This position will become clearer as I unravel my contentions in the debate. The literature needs a different approach. There is a need for a deep lecture on the issues that characterize the current debate.

The views I will echo in this manuscript have compiled hoping they might help shine a projector on the

---

1. The term "L'Hexagone" is the informal name of France (also known as "La France"). The country is commonly known as the French Republic or La République Française. The country is formerly known as the "Gaule."

issues that have dominated the literature for many years. The aim is to examine, up close, popular disagreements that form enthusiastic discussions either in favor or against Sartre. My position is distinct, for the aim is to look at these issues antithetically. The next pages outline that approach further.

PROVOKING A GENUINE DEBATE

To clarify the crux of the debate against Jean-Paul Sartre, there is a need to highlight misguided claims about the man and his works. Critics are quick to challenge the works Sartre produced by evoking dubious claims about his intellectual application. Rarely do critics impute Sartre a culpability of some sort for his presumed failure to be a great philosopher. Their criticism of the man, I would contend, is partly because he is a brilliant thinker.

Critics seldom examine the works Sartre produced with glee or with a positive mindset. It is all about debunking Sartre; it is all about outlining his literary flaws. There is a need to change that reality.

It is important to point out a few inaccurate criticisms of Sartre. The hope is that you will understand the origin of the arguments that are often legislated against Sartre to lessen his intellectual relevance in the ethical discipline.

The notion that Sartre played a substantive role in ethics has been debated extensively. The consensus is that Sartre was not a moral philosopher. That claim does not invite any agreement. How might one support such a position without a shred of a doubt? You might find a potential answer in my other treats on the subject. For now, let us glance at the essence of the issues that are often levied in the literature.

There is enough reason to be curious about the singularity of the dispute against Sartre. However, we must be cautious.

There is a deliberate want to undermine Sartrean philosophy. Despite the intricate nature of the debate, the facts are readily available.

The reality of the works Sartre produced can be overwhelming. Keep an open mind as you navigate this work. It is important to uphold a positive outlook as you make your way through the remaining part of the text.

It is vital to have a frank debate about Sartre. A sound analysis of the issues would change the course of the debate; it would change the tone of the conversation; it would allow a better assessment of Sartre (as an extraordinary thinker) and his works in ethics or in philosophy. It may be urgent to satisfy your intellectual curiosity about Sartre.

Despite it all, there are enough reasons to defend the Sartrean ethical model. To fulfill the mentioned goals, this work sketches out the debate as coherent as possible. The goal is to offer a bird's-eye view of the debate and highlight my position about the subject.[2]

Another aim in compiling this work is to help you make sense of the issues. It is likely that you might disagree with the views expressed here. I don't think it is important that you share my passion for defending Sartre. The goal is to outline the arguments to incite you to reflect on whether Sartre's treatment in the literature is fair or whether such a treatment is unjust. The next section clarifies the issues further.

CHANGING THE CONVERSATION

The expectation was that the positions echoed in this text might help stir the debate in the proper direction. Sartre

[2]. I use this term to depict the burdensome work I went through to compile this book.

deserves recognition in the ethical genre. Sartre played a role in moral philosophy, although many of his works were not tailored to ethics. He contributed to ontology and ethics.

While most observers disagree that Sartre played a significant role in ethics, there are inconsistencies in the debate. Such drawbacks are worthy of further analysis in the present context. Criticisms can be unfair in their approaches of the work that Sartre produced both while alive and the work released posthumously.

The belief is that Sartre did not lay a solid foundation for his ethics in the works he published while alive and posthumously. Although this understanding might be true, there is more to Sartrean ethics than most would admit. We should not deny Sartre a role in this discipline, even though Sartre's work on ethics might not be perfect. These writings are not devoid of intellectual relevance. There is a need to recognize a Sartrean role in the ethical domain.

My contention may not affect the literature positively. My arguments may not be heard; they may not be taken seriously. I would not still echo that Sartre deserves consideration as a moral philosopher.

SARTRE DESERVES BETTER

Why does Sartre deserve better? One way to put it is that Sartre deserves proper credit for his work on ethics. Challenges against Sartre in this domain hardly have a legitimate claim against the role the man played in the discipline. It is necessary to reexamine popular accounts against Sartre.

The following five reasons mat help clarify that reality. First, the conversation is one-sided. As a result, there is a need to highlight a different side of Jean-Paul Sartre. Second, criticisms against Sartre are weak. There is a need for sound evidence to support the idea that Sartre was not a moral philosopher. The argument could be made that Sartre developed a relevant ethical analysis in his work. He echoed similar positions in his publications about human ontology. Third, the Sartrean view of morality could be best explored through a different lens. Existing criticisms are not based on the work of Sartre produced in the domain. Fourth, criticisms against Sartre are unnecessary. There is a bitterness towards the man. Because of this atmosphere of hostility, Sartre's ideas are challenged, all too often, without methodical deliberations. Fifth, there is a need to reexamine the conflict that exists between Sartre and his most avid detractors. It is vital to understand the man; it is also paramount to grasp the nature of the contestations, which symbolizes the debate.

Criticism of the Sartrean approach to morality is often based on an obscurantist examination of the works he produced. Disagreements often devalue the Sartrean intellectual valor. As a philosopher or even as a writer, Sartre receives little or no credit for his contribution to ethical writings. Sartre is treated as a literary punching bag. Everyone has something negative to say about Sartre.

There is a need to capture the essence of the debate trying to challenge the role that Sartre is thought to have played in ethics. It is important to explore the reason some people offer to justify their aversion against the essentiality of Sartrean ethics. It is vital to assess parts of the disputes, which are often designed to rebuke Sartre, if not to destroy the man as a worthy writer.

Sartre is a philosopher of history. There is a need to examine the basis of popular criticisms against him. There is a need to explore claims that are routinely echoed to refute

Sartre as a fine intellectual. There is a need to outline why a better approach toward Sartre is necessary.

There is a need to accept Sartre's significance. Doing so might help us grasp the extent of human experience. Criticisms against Sartre, notably his approach to ethics, are biased; thus, they are prejudicial to Sartre's true literary valor. Many criticisms, which had been designed specifically to disagree with Sartre, are unwarranted. These criticisms seldom consider that Sartre developed an ethic in his major philosophical works.

That does not mean that Sartre was perfect. That does not even presume that the Sartrean model of philosophy was flawless. While some stands against Sartre might be called for much sensible approach might also be of a need. Although we could not claim that the works Sartre produced are in perfect state, we could not deny them altogether based on our subjective interpretations of their intrinsic valor. Criticisms against Sartre should be guided by an understanding of the issues at hand. Such rebuttals must be more sensible or much healthier, at least in the intellectual realm, than they are now.

The Sartrean approach to ethics is not perfect. Although his arguments might be incomplete, that should not deny the relevance of Sartrean ethics. You might not be a follower of the Sartrean model. That does not mean that you should be an anti-Sartre. You might accept Sartre's valor in the ethical discipline, although his works might have a few defects.

6. ASSESSING WHY SARTRE LIVES ON

A little over one hundred and ten years ago, Jean-Paul Sartre was born (1905). It has also been over 40 years since he passed away (1980–2022). Based on the "one-century-per-genie" archetype referenced in the earlier section, the year that marked Sartre's 100th birthday (for example, 2005) should have been the end of his reign in human literature. That year resulted in a spike of interest for Sartrean writings.[1]

Between 2005 and 2006, Hazel Rowley published both the English and the French versions of a remarkable, if not a provocative, piece of literature about Sartre and Simone de Beauvoir.[2] Sartre and Beauvoir are among the most well-known voices of modern existentialism.[3] They are often the subject of criticisms and unflattering inquiries.

Few critics spared Sartre in their wrath of "obiter dicta." He has been the subject of tittle-tattles. Both Sartre's personal

---

[1]. Between 2005 to this day, several authors have explored Jean-Paul Sartre and his philosophy. Several literary works had been produced about Jean-Paul Sartre between 2005 and 2006.

[2]. Hazel Rowley published the French version in 2006. It was published by Gillamard. The English version was published by Harper Collins in 2005, in the United States.

[3]. The book was translated in English in 2006.

and professional activities are treated as public domains. His troubles and his dirty laundry are revealed in the public square.

A CHARACTER ASSASSINATION

The argument could be made that most criticisms against Sartre amount to character assassination. Rowley's book about Sartre and de Beauvoir should fall into this category. The author gave credence to the preceding assertions in facets of the book titled *Tête-à-tête Simone de Beauvoir and Jean-Paul Sartre*. The book had negatively awakened public interest in Sartre and Beauvoir several years after their death. The paperback placed Sartre under the radar of popular criticism.

The revelations in Rowley's book were damaging to the reputation of both Sartre and de Beauvoir. These individuals, Rowley suggests, are much more wicked than previously thought. The publication also sparked a long-standing debate about the convincingness of a widely guessed romantic affair between Sartre and Beauvoir. Rowley revealed that the pair had an open-ended romantic bond. This was a "contingency relationship" that resulted in a series of love affairs and sexual involvement with various third-party lovers.

According to Rowley, it was a "Ménage à trois" lasting between Sartre, Beauvoir, and his current lover. The third-party lover was unaware of the deceitful nature of both Sartre and Beauvoir; he or she was constantly being manipulated by this existentialist duo. During this sexual experiment, the person represented "une victime qui doit être immolée" or a victim who must be sacrificed.

Rowley's book further suggested that Beauvoir and Sartre had crafted a meticulous plan, if not a wicked strategy, to enjoy each other's company sexually and intellectually. They would engage in romantic relations with other individuals on the side.

Beauvoir was "Sartre's pimp" (McEwen and Ellmann 2006). This was a scandalous affair, which generated much attention both in the literary world and in various social circles.

The collective understanding is that Beauvoir would seduce a young woman, often a young girl, preferably in her teen years, and she (that is, Beauvoir) would later introduce her new lover to Sartre. Sartre would breed a romantic rapport with Beauvoir's new romantic conquest (Fraser 1999).[4] It was also understood that Beauvoir had many types of lovers, including men and women.

It is widely believed that Sartre was interested in Beauvoir's young female lovers. Observers argued that Sartre was a "coureur de jupons" or a "womanizer." Even during Sartre's later years in life, he had many lovers on the side. Therefore, the view is that Sartre had no problem letting Simone de Beauvoir see other women and even other men (McEwen and Ellmann 2006).

REBUKING SARTRE

The work by Rowley was, without fail, not a flattery publication about the duo. Across many circles, it drew many praises, but fewer, if any at all, condemnations. The book condemned both Sartre and Beauvoir as liars and depraved human beings. Rowley's writing also suggested the pair had no actual sense of moral decency and had little or no regard for the well-being of their sexual victims.

---

[4]. Beauvoir's bisexuality is amply discussed in "Identity Without Selfhood: Simone de Beauvoir and bisexuality. Mariam Fraser frames Beauvoir as a sexually ambivalent. The author notes that Beauvoir was not so much a lesbian; she enjoyed different-sex relationship.

Although the book was critical of the pair, some commentators were shocked at what they described as Rowley's soft approach to debauchery, which for many years had been rumored about this power couple in the French literature. Rowley reviewed an array of personal letters that Sartre and Beauvoir had written and addressed to one another.

Rowley consulted letters, which the pair (supposedly) wrote to third-party individuals. Her accounts suggest that these letters were interesting and shocking. The understanding is that these letters confirmed what many people had been whispering in dark alleys about these existentialists.

The previously noted paperback is among the many publications that have helped cast doubts about the moral virtue of both Sartre and Beauvoir. Rowley inferred that, while the pair had been known publicly as some of the smartest people in France, though Sartre and de Beauvoir had different ideals in their views on the relationship among ethics, desire, and gender (Gothlin 1999), they had also been living double lives. Rowley took it on herself to reveal what she saw as the dark side of both Sartre and Beauvoir.

Rowley's book suggested the couple's public life was professedly well choreographed to project an image of sanctity and an incommensurable amount of intellectual puritanism. Their private lifestyle, often more immoral than might have been visible to most, was—in fact—filled with deceitful practices and marked by morally distasteful conducts. The pair was engulfed in dramas and romantic shenanigans, glaringly with previous lovers (McEwen and Ellmann 2006).

Other observers noted that Rowley's book was not so much a biography of Sartre and Beauvoir. To a certain extent, it was a revelatory piece of literature which unmasked the genuine characters of these sonorously sexually liberal intellectuals. Although Rowley's writings on Sartre and Beauvoir had a gossipy character and little or no academic value, the publication was well received in various settings. The book had been cited a few times in several scholarly works.

A few dissenters regretted that Rowley did not seek to examine how the shadowy lives, which these two personalities had lived, might have affected their professional lives, including their writings. Todd McEwen and Lucy Ellmann exclaimed: "Rowley's readings of their novels are overly literal: There are more urgent things to say about them than which protégé was portrayed as which character" (McEwen and Ellmann 2006).

Other than the "juicy titbits" that Rowley exposed about Sartre, the year 2005 (later years as well) symbolized the publication of an array of articles, blog posts, and magazines about Sartre. The problem is that many of these works rebuked Sartre both personally and intellectually. During that time, there were books released on Sartre. Most works on Sartre have been excessively critical of his philosophical approach, namely his take on subjectivity. The Sartrean approach to human morality has also been under intense scrutiny.

Despite the negative effects of Rowley's popular book, I interpret her writings from a different angle. The book showed that Sartre's presence is still memorable among us. Sartre's thoughts, unaccountably, his views on human ethics and ontology, are still relevant to human literature. The Sartrean way of assessing human morality continues to linger in many philosophical debates.

Through fervent criticisms, Sartre's works, be they on philosophy or on ethics, are still relevant in popular culture. Thus, the Sartrean legacy lives on. Jean-Paul Sartre lives on.

A RELEVANT THINKER IN ETHICS

Sartre is still a relevant thinker. Despite his death, he is still a significant contributor to modern philosophy. The same is manifestly true in his approach to ethics. The challenge is to highlight this relevance as clearly as possible.

Sartre was a philosopher. Similarly, he was an unparalleled thinker. Thus, Sartre lives on and will continue to be that way in modern-day literature. These facts are rarely contested.

Many commentators have pointed out that Sartre was a tremendously organized writer. Other observers also viewed him as a systematic intellectual (Linsenbard 2000). Some people will vouch for Sartre as a moral philosopher. What might explain that?

As opposed to popular beliefs, Sartre played a significant role in the ethical discipline. The goal (be it unrealistic or chimerical) is to outline this role compellingly. Sartre often outlined his ethical concerns in an unambiguous format.

The Sartrean assessments of the extent of human morality are thereabouts obvious throughout his works. This is the case uniquely if we were to pay closer attention to both his writing style and the way he often sets up his argumentation (Linsenbard 2000). These facts are rarely recognized in positive terms. It is important to examine the context of the treatments that Sartre received as he is both physically and mentally unavailable to defend his ideas.[5]

---

[5]. What I am suggesting is that Sartre passed away a long time ago. Yet, countless works have looked to undermine his role in moral philosophy. Sartre cannot defend his views. Criticisms seem directed at only other critics. The sad reality is that most criticisms are similar. I question their relevance.

SECTION THREE

Unparalleled Contempt

7. SARTRE AND THE HATERS

What is it about Jean-Paul Sartre that made him such an important player in modern-day literature? It might be impossible to answer this question short of encouraging slight towards Sartre. The challenge might be to find a means to make my case without encouraging others to question my position. It is undisputable that Sartre is examined incomparably to other public figures in philosophy.

Sartrean writings are well studied. Yet, there is still a need to talk about Sartre. There is always an avid interest in deciphering the Sartrean model of exploring human morality. In both academic and in other settings, Sartre is always the subject of intense scrutiny. What would be the reason (or reasons) which might explain that reality?

While answers are not clear, it is well documented that Sartre is constantly under examination; and that for assorted reasons. He is unquestionably the most criticized thinker of the last century. Istvan Meszaros, for instance, notes "No writer in his lifetime has been the target of so many attacks, from the most varied and rather powerful quarters" (Meszaros 2012, 15).

Who could defend Sartre against the many ill-fated critiques that, by most accounts, pollute the conversation? The question is who could do that effectively? What is certain is that it would not be Sartre.

As a deceased philosopher, Sartre can no longer defend against ill-conceived criticisms. Who could do it? The answer about whom it could be could also become elusive.

No one seems interested in taking on this task; there are no declared contenders to care for the Sartrean ethical legacy. To defend Sartre, the expert, one would have to show great intellectual bravery. Few people could make such a claim without being dismissed at once.

Based on the earlier observations, it could be said that Sartre is among the few writers who have provoked so much scorn even beyond the grave. Sartre is criticized as if he were a newcomer to the field of philosophy. Sartrean writings are often examined as if they had entered the literary stream recently. Until now, Sartre has continued to be the subject of staunch criticisms.

A MAGNET FOR CRITICISM

Jean-Paul Sartre attracted many types of criticism. Most disparages against him have been destructive. Again, what would explain (or what could justify) this reality? In fact, the answers are not resolved.

What was the reason that Sartre stood for a magnet for criticisms? Why was he so despised? Why did people find it easier to rebuff his views, rather than embracing them?

These are excellent questions. As suggested earlier, there is also a lack of succinct answers about the reason (or the reasons) most people had little or no tolerance for Sartre. The motives or potential motives for hating Sartre are not always clear.

I do not offer answers to these questions. This work was not designed to inquire about the underlying cause for the obvious anti-Sartre sentiment that pervades the literature. The need to look at Sartre differently is there. It may be up to us to examine the existing criticisms of Sartre. There is a need to do so both inside and out.

I could theorize about the reason (or potential reasons) Sartre incited so many dissenting reviews. Let us examine, at least speculatively here, the grounds on which Sartre earned so many haters. A conceivable observation, which might explain sides of the preceding questions, is that Sartre spearheaded a marked change in the way human beings could examine themselves in their environment. The intellectual optics proposed by Sartre (for example, through existentialism), to examine the man, have never been substituted by a more potent literary tool or a more significant intellectual instrument. A worthy argument is that there is a resentment or a "jalousie" against Sartre.

Sartre's philosophical writings are often debated, criticized, dismissed, and considered incendiary by most observers. During his career, Sartre questioned the wisdom of popular ideas, which have had a significant impact on human existence since the dawn of time. Most people did not like Sartre for his argumentative tone alone.

Faced with Sartre's popularity and intellectual brilliance, he was never considered the darling of philosophy. While alive, his views were often condemned. While deceased, his hard-earned reputation is often smeared, as in countless published works, feigning him personally and rebuking his rapport with Simone de Beauvoir.

The literature is filled with works that are critical of Sartre. In my view, these works have little or no academic relevance.[1] They are usually well made up and aptly written to rebuke Sartre and to poke holes in his major theories. His writings are belittled or set aside at any hint of argumentative flaws.

The rise of modern technology did not bode well for Sartre and the Sartrean legacy. Criticisms could not define a domain. Anyone could criticize Sartre. Many have done so with no restraint or denial. The Internet, for instance, is filled with works that look to devalue Sartre, although there are a few other entities that often praise the Sartrean contributions to human literature in the cyberspace.

The work explained earlier by Hazel Rowley falls within that category; at least, it does so ostensibly. We must explore the identity of this thinker. We must explore the hatred that many people felt or still feel for Sartre.

It is worth asking this question again. Who was Sartre from a philosophical lens? Are criticisms against him are correct? Are dissenting views against Sartre's philosophy relevant? Let us explore Sartre's philosophical identity.

A MARXIST BY CONVENIENCE

Karl Marx is credited with saying that "religion is the opium of the people." By that view, it is sure sounds like people, notably the masses, need religion to quench their yearning for social equity. It could also be foreshadowed that religion serves as a buffer, which prevents ordinary folks from questioning the

---

[1]. There are works that are based on opinions, which are not necessarily academic. Such works are not always supported by research or empirical data.

sanctity of the world as they know it. This understanding could be misguided.

This quote about the Marxist ideal is often taken out of context. It suggests that Karl Marx hated religion. Contrary to popular assumptions, this quotation is the snippet of a longer and more intense articulation, which Karl Marx reflected about the role of religion in society.[2] It is probable that Karl Marx looked to suggest an oxymoronic view about the need for a deity in a social milieu.

Austin Cline notes that "Marx offers a partial validation of religion because it tries to become the heart of a heartless world" (Cline 2019). Karl Marx also suggested that religion was a drag. He argues, "Religion is one form of spiritual oppression which everywhere weighs down heavily upon the masses of the people, overburdened by their perpetual work for others, by want and isolation" (Marx 2001, 8). In his major works, Karl Marx argues both in favor and against the need for religion in the world.

In the beginning of his professional life, Sartre was a committed Marxist. Over the years, Sartre took the notion of religion, as explained by Karl Marx, to an extreme level. Throughout his career, Sartre struck an important nerve within various religious circles.

Existentialism is inherently "anti-God." Sartre argues that there is no God; there is no destiny. As a result, the individual must constantly try to build himself from the ground and up

---

[2]. Karl Marx said more than just, "Religion is the opium of the masses." A more extended version of the quote reads like this, "Religious distress is at the same time the expression of real distress and the protest real distress. Religion is the sigh of the oppressed creature, the heart of a heartless world, just as it is the spirit of a spiritless situation. It is the opium of the people. Karl Marx, *Critique of Hegel's Philosophy of Rights* (1844).

in the world. People who espoused certain dogmatic beliefs, ill-conceived notions, or those who held misguided ideological views nourished little appreciation for Sartrean writings.

People who disagreed with Sartre have often looked to discredit him both personally and intellectually. Dissenters tried to tarnish the Sartrean legacy at every opportunity they had. Some observers have tarnished his reputation in any way imaginable.

For the Sartrean mindset about morality and human freedom, the collective understanding is that Sartre got it wrong. For most observers, freedom and ethics are incompatible; they are that way both theoretically and concretely. Dissenters have argued that Sartre contradicts himself when he tries to settle the two ideas. The disunity in the debate centers on the viewpoint that, if the man must strive to be free, there could be no ethics.

There is an economic reason worth considering. Sartre was a staunch opponent of several theories, which have had an enormous impact on human existence; at least, it was that way from an economic lens. Sartre also became disenchanted with the Marxist ideology, at least toward the end of his career.

As Sartre reached a certain intellectual growth and philosophical maturity, he was a bit more radical. As he proved in his own ideas about the need for individual freedom, he also became estranged from Marxist ideals or ideas. Sartre was not fond of Marxism toward the end of his life or at the twilight of his intellectual career.

Sartre was decided about the role of his existentialist ideals of enlightening the man. He was vocal against the effects of Communism; he despised the weight of capitalism on the man; he bemoaned the reach of colonialism in society. Sartre was fixed against colonialist practices, reputably in Africa (for example, Algeria).[3]

The ideas Sartre echoed during his prolific writing career represent a menace to oligarchs all over the world. That might explain why his scrutiny of the man within the environment is disputed. That is the reason his view of the individual in the world or within the social environment is rebuffed without mercy.

---

[3] To learn more about this understanding, see the book titled Jean-Paul Sartre and Morality. See (Johnson 2017, 12).

8. A THREAT TO SOCIETY

Despite criticisms, which are aimed at Jean-Paul Sartre, at least in several corners, Sartrean writings are regarded as a positive contribution to human literature. In contrast, the Sartrean approach to various philosophical ideas is not intellectually relevant. This view is motivated by political reasons.

In a few circles, both Sartre and his philosophy are rebuffed. Sartre was viewed as a threat to the status quo. Sartre's theorem about human relations in the world was often contextualized as a major threat to society.

The Sartrean ideals, one could make the case, effectively threatened the foundation of society or social arrangements during his epoch. Sartre, not necessarily his works, was viewed as a problem by most people, notably those in a position of power. It could be said that Sartre was regarded as a menace to the societal status quo of his era.

The Sartrean "critique" of the world or his harsh assessments of social environments were not consistent or correct, at least not all the time. The Sartrean model to understanding the extent of human existence was demagogic and, at other times, trendsetting. Critics overlook the positive sides of Sartrean thoughts and focus only on the negative ramifications that could be inferred from those inquiries. I do not share a similar approach to Sartre's works.

The way Sartre studied the human project could be considered both revolutionary. His prescriptions for achieving social freedom hinge on the need for a revolutionary transformation in both the individual and the environment (that is, the setting where the man evolves). Sartre wanted an eternal revolution in the man, which would undermine social order and social structure (that is, social institutions).

It is irrefutable that a thinker like Sartre would almost attract an incommensurable number of criticisms. Such a thinker would be dreaded by many social groups. Indeed, Sartre was despised in various social settings. To echo an earlier claim, Sartre is smeared on many sides, including his personal life and his academic efforts.

AN INTELLECTUAL REBEL

Sartre was regarded as an intellectual rebel. Indeed, his view of the world was distinct. His method was genuine.

Sartre examined human conditions contrary to the way most thinkers had been examining the human project. Sartre differed from other thinkers; his approach was genuine; his views were intellectually overpowering.

It is undeniable that Sartre was an outlier; he was an altruist. Sartre was also a pioneer in the field known as phenomenology. For these reasons, it is likely that Sartre attracted criticisms expressly because his ideas were novel. Intellectuals had a tough time accepting the Sartrean analytical model. Observers were startled by the Sartrean worldviews. They hated Sartre for all the wrong reasons.

Sartre was not easily intimidated by criticism. He often espoused a condescending attitude towards his critics. Sartre spared no one who did not spare him. He was feisty. He was relentless in his attacks towards his staunch critics.

Despite the many disparagements that characterize Sartre's works, the Sartrean imprint on literature is still plain to see. His philosophical notions, his fierce debates about morality, have remained the preferable medium through which to understand the extent of being in nature or society. It is also best to assess the nature of human conduct in the world.

As most observers, though they are a handful, often note, Sartre is alive and well by his writings. In other works, I note the Sartrean legacy lives on. I am sure that this legacy will endure despite the rise of disparagements against Sartre.

Critics have bombarded the literature with works that looked to rebuke Sartre's relevance as both an existentialist and a moralist. Opponents weaken Sartre's intellectual worth; more obviously, they undermine his impetus in ethics. The question worth asking here is why this is the case.

The motives that some critics might have had in mind for rejecting the Sartrean slant to ethics are not clear. The reason his view on several issues is rebuffed in the literature is not always obvious. My view is that morality is the foundation of the Sartrean philosophical trademark.

Ethics were among the subjects. Many critics refuse to concede Sartre a spot or any recognition. Was it by coincidence, or was it by design? One may find it difficult to come up with an irrefutable answer.

Sartre had a significant vulnerability. In one of his major works about the roots of human ontology (for example, in the book titled *Being and Nothingness*), Sartre made a promise to his readers (Warnock 1966). As he used the notions of "for-itself" and "in-itself" to describe two modalities of being (Williams 2015), Sartre unequivocally promised to work on ethics

(Crittenden 1998). The promised work was supposed to center on the link between the moral problems, as he conceived such impediments, with his approach to phenomenological ontology (Linsenbard 2000). Most observers consider this promise as the tipping point in Sartre's decadence.

In the previously noted publication, Sartre promised to dedicate his future writing projects to ethics. He promised to examine the man (or the being) on the ethical plane. Sartre never concretized this goal, at least while alive.

Sartre did not publish a book that clearly said his positions on certain ethical issues. However, he published such work postmortem. Here, the understanding is that Sartre's most popular works in the field had been published posthumously. That fact, as we gather, does not explain why a Sartrean tactic to examining human morality is excessively contested.

Could we consider Sartre's failure to publish his own ethics troubling? Should it matter whether Sartre published his own work or whether someone published them on his behalf? The answer could be no. Let us explore this facet of the debate.

FAILURE TO HONOR HIS PROMISE

The illogicality that Sartre did not honor his promise to compile a book on ethics is purely conjectural. This should have little or no intellectual weight in shaming Sartre's literary legacy. Whether Sartre honored a promise should not be considered as a practical instrument for gauging his intellectual potency in ethics.

The reality of criticism toward Sartre on this front can be demoralizing. From many points of view, Jean-Paul Sartre fell short of honoring his pledge to his readers or to the public. For most observers, this failure was fatal to Sartre's relevance in the ethical genre. The cause of this failure is not always clear.

Suppose that we were to agree that Sartre had been a failure in moral philosophy; it might still be difficult to make similar claims in other works or with other literary works, which Sartre aimed for. There are good reasons for the failure in the ethical discipline. Adrian van den Hoven notes the postwar era was hectic for Sartre (Hoven and Leak 2005).

Sartre was distracted by several issues that were political. He was busy traveling and had to attend his duties toward the journal Les Temps Modernes, which he founded (Hoven and Leak 2005). Although this might be true, no one could make excuses for the expert. We could examine this issue differently.

The literature is filled with ill-conceived criticisms about Sartre and his works. If critics were not so entrenched in dissecting ethics to a point where little or nothing is left of the core ideas, Sartre explained, they might see that he honored his pledge. Sartre has a publication that directly addresses his ethical concerns; it is titled *Cahiers pour une morale* (in the French version) or *Notebooks for an Ethics* (in the English).

Sartre produced several notebooks, which outlined his most vivid ethical concerns. Until the 1990s, most of the materials in those notebooks had not been revealed to the public. Many of Sartre's posthumous works in the ethical domain include transcripts of lectures, which he gave in the past or lectures that he was preparing to give before passing away. This is well known in the literature. It would not be misplaced or even condescending to say that most critics are not always genuine when they argue that Sartre produced little or no relevant works on ethics.

If critics had looked at Sartre's works holistically, they could have recognized the mere fact that Sartre published a book on the subject is enough proof that the man did not abandon his search to develop a solid ethical examination of his philosophy. We could debate by far the weight of the Sartrean slant on ethics. Denying his contribution or challenging the role of his works on ethics seems hasty.

Sartre's work on ethics came out after he died. The ideas he echoed seemed disjoint, at least to some authorities in the ethical discipline. The fact remains that Sartre examined the man on the ethical plane, at least as he promised (Anderson 2002b). For unsophisticated observers, for people like me, Sartre's notebooks do not cardinally portray a shallow picture of his approach to human morality, as critics usually argue.

Another angle to consider is that Sartre had been working on a few notes, lectures, and manuscripts, which were theoretically tailored for ethics.[1] As implied above, Sartre had been working exhaustingly to compile his ethical ideas on or around the time that he passed away. Sartre compiled several works that offer an obvious hint of his stance on ethics at once.

The extent of these works is discussed in depth in the text titled *Sartrean Ethics* (released in 2016), which I referenced earlier in the present manuscript. I have addressed sides of this question in the text titled *Jean-Paul Sartre and Morality* (released in 2017). Most of the works Sartre produced about ethics were not literary novelties. Many of these accomplishments had been in the making shortly after his major publication, discussing the crux of existentialism.

Evidence shows that Sartre did not abandon his wish to study the man on the ethical plane. There is enough evidence as well to suggest that he delayed his ethics-related works for other projects, including the text titled *Being and Nothingness*. For sure, let us explore that likelihood in more detail. The next chapter will dive deeper into this well-known likelihood.

---

[1] To learn more about this idea, see (Johnson 2016). You may also see: (Johnson 2016, 74–80)

SECTION 4

Jean-Paul Sartre and His Drawbacks

9. DELAYING HIS OWN WORKS

Was Jean-Paul Sartre hesitant about publishing his works on ethics? Did he delay intentionally his work on ethics? We could guess about answers. This prospect is not that far off.

Sartre's promise of *Being and Nothingness* was not an empty pledge. He intended to examine the person on the ethical plane. Arguably, Sartre reached that goal when he published a book describing his ethical stance. A reference is the notebooks that Sartre published postmortem.

Beyond question, Sartre did not publish the book, as most of his fans expected. We could claim the reason he did not honor his promise was independent of his true intents. Extraneous circumstances impeded Sartre from honoring his pledge while alive. It should not matter whether Sartre published his works or whether someone else did it on his behalf.

Despite the view that Sartre is a failure in ethics because he did not honor his promise, there is enough evidence to support the notion that he fulfilled that commitment, at least partially. Sartre intended to examine the person (the being) on the ethical plane. Sartre did so eloquently in his notebooks. But critics might disagree.

Sartre compiled some important works on ethics. One could make the case that the Sartrean legacy is well settled in this domain. Do not just rely on my assertions. It might not make sense to consider myself the only one who sees the Sartrean legacy in ethical writings in this way.

Other iconoclasts share a similar sentiment about the origins of Sartrean ethics. A prominent author in the field (Thomas Anderson) notes that Sartre promised to write about authenticity, a cardinal notion in Sartre's early ethics. Anderson argues that Sartre honored this promise around the 1940s, though he never published the works (Anderson 2002b, 138). Although this is just one example. Most observers agree with Anderson.

It is also worth outlining that there are those who are not convinced of Sartre's role in ethics. These critics have treated Sartre's apparent (or perceived) failure to express his own ethical views as a great faux pas. They used this as a pretext to undermine Sartre's literary legacy.

Other critics have treated this detail as a testament to Sartre's contribution to philosophy. This is not a fair portrayal of Sartre's contribution to the ethical genre. This is an inaccurate depiction of Sartre's overall role in the human literature.

There is more to Sartre's true intellectual worse than most critics would admit. This is the essence of my disappointment in the conversation on Sartre. The nature of Sartre's ethical works is not a puzzle, as most critics portray it to be.

SARTRE'S TRUE INTELLECTUAL WORTH

In this volume, I adopted a different approach. I argue in contrast to the way Sartre's true intellectual valor is depicted in the literature. I have espoused a similar slant for the role Sartre played in ethics. For these reasons, I am convinced there is more to Sartrean ethics than relegating that ethics to a mere failed promise or presuming that.

In ethics, my position is obvious. It is ideal to explore the power of Sartre's writings from all angles. Such a method might not be that simple. To achieve that goal, I propose a comprehensive method. This is the best way to examine the nature of Sartre's works on ethics. This is the best way to end reservations about Sartrean ethics.

Although Sartre produced an array of materials that address his ethical concerns, critics often—hastily, I might add—rebuffed the utility of such works. They usually label them as rambling, disjointed, abstract, and incomplete. Most observers consider Sartre's final works, whether they had been tinted for ethics, unfinished, and fragmented.

For most critics, such works are inadequate to give Sartre a voice in the field. That view sound misguided. I have striven rigorously to rebuke this understanding. I have done so passionately in my other works.

Even though many of the works that Sartre produced about moral philosophy were unfinished, that would not imply they have little or no literary value. Sartre recognized that most of his ideas were not finished.[1] He noted that he abandoned these materials, though he intended to complete them in the future.

To express this view, Sartre made a deliberate choice to leave his work on ethics. He intended to complete them later. Sartre thought that he could do so as time allowed. Some observers have also echoed that, even though Sartre

---

[1] To learn more about this idea, see (Johnson 2016)

abandoned his notebooks for an ethic, clearly the concerns stayed with him (Hoven and Leak 2005).

Every hint suggests that Sartre recognized his drawbacks in the ethical genre. He admitted that his works were incomplete. The question is whether this is enough to rebuke Sartre in the field. That being recognized, I must note that other observers might beg to differ.

For a few critics, Sartre's own admission is proof that even he had little or no faith in his ability to produce an ethical theory worthy of his intellectual brilliance. This was to the contrary. This likelihood would not or should not set up a formal basis on which to deny the weight or even disagree with the applicability of Sartre's works on ethics.

ARGUMENTS AGAINST JEAN-PAUL SARTRE

Does Sartre deserve any recognition as a moral philosopher? Depending on whom you ask that question, getting a succinct answer could be in the negative. There is a litany of arguments in the literature against Sartre. Often, such arguments are meticulously framed to rebuke him. In this context, I will only address a few of them.

Differences of opinion towards the extent of Sartrean ethics are not always brief. Many scholars disagree with the idea that Sartre could have a legitimate claim to moral philosophy. Richard Bernstein notes, "In his popular pamphlet, L'Existentialisme est un humanisme, Sartre attempted to outline the ethics he promised at the end of Being and Nothingness" (Bernstein 2011, 153). Yet, the Sartrean approach to ethics has more rhetoric than substance, Bernstein argues (Bernstein 2011).

For Richard Bernstein, Sartre could not prove himself as a moral philosopher. To what extent is this understanding true? One may lack clarity on how to approach this question without appearing being haughty. Bernstein's argument sounds vengeful, if I may say so, and intellectually meritless, though I would not call his slant dishonest on the outset.

There is no mystery in Sartrean ethics. Suggesting otherwise is bad faith or ignorance, though one may lack a clear understanding of which is more fitting to describe Bernstein's approach. There is not a standard for being a moral philosopher. Bernstein could not be the gatekeeper of such a road to ethics even if it were to exist. His assessment of Sartre's works is simply a deflection of his own intellectual failing in moral philosophy.

As already suggested throughout this paperback, Sartre authored many literary publications about his tactic to decipher his ethical concerns. The common belief centers on the view that these works lack the essential part of a sound analytical approach to ethics. This is a subjective interpretation of these works.

The argument that Sartre is not a moral philosopher lacks credence. It could not compel any sound-minded individual to share a similar sentiment based on the evidence presented. The next chapter offers a reason to support this rebuke of some of the most pervasive arguments against Sartre.

10. EXAMINING THE ARGUMENTS

Three specific arguments are often levied to rebuke Sartrean ethics, though not in the precise language in which I outline them in this work.[1] The later paragraphs offer an outline of these points of view. I encourage you to read the book entitled *Sartrean Ethics* to learn more about these arguments.[2]

The first point of disagreement centers on the contribution Sartre made to ethics. I refer to this view as "The Publication Argument."[3] From this angle, the debate is tilted towards a scrutiny of the works Sartre published. Keep in mind that this is not a correct examination of the quality of those works.

Most observers argue that Sartre did not make any important contribution to the ethical domain. The argument is that Sartre only published one book about the subject, and,

---

[1]. The arguments against Jean-Paul Sartre are legion. They are scattered in various forms throughout the literature. For the sake of simplicity, I have synthesized them in three major arguments: publication, substance, and theoretical.

[2] To learn more about this idea, see (Johnson 2016). You may also see: (Johnson 2016, 60–67).

[3] To learn more about this idea, see (Johnson 2016). You may also see: (Johnson 2016, 61).

because of his absence, no one had any chance to ask him directly about his works or the aptness of the views he expressed. The presumption is that such works are not suitable for allowing Sartre any relevance in the ethical domain. That position is mistaken.

The preceding arguments against the works which Sartre produced seldom consider the intellectual importance of these compilations in the ethical discipline. Sartre's posthumous works, with his other publications, frame an undisputable body of information on his approach to ethics.

The notion that the works Sartre produced about ethics are incomplete does not consider his compilations about human existence, which have an irrefutable link with morality. This view overlooks the intellectual worth of both published and unpublished works that Sartre produced on ethics. This is an inaccurate slant seeking to undermine the Sartrean literary legacy. This is an unjustified assault on Sartre and his intellectual valor in ethics.

The complete rejection of the intellectual utility of the works Sartre produced about ethics, both while alive and posthumously does not seem fair. It is unquestionable that, since Sartre passed away, he published many materials related to ethics by his daughter, Arlette Elkaïm-Sartre. On Sartre's passing, Elkaïm-Sartre became his sole literary "executrix" (Lloyd and Fornasiero 2014). Under that authority, Elkaïm-Sartre published several written materials, which Sartre had conferred to her care.

It is accepted that the works, which Elkaïm-Sartre released on Sartre's behalf, are genuine. These works are, in fact, Sartre's intellectual productions. Rejecting them could only be a way to denigrate Sartre.

The second point at issue examines the essence (or the substance) of the works that Sartre produced but did not publish while alive. This view could be described as "the substance argument." Here, the debate centers on the essentiality or nature of the works that Sartre compiled.

Critics complain that these bits and pieces of ideas lack substance and lack materiality. The stand inferred from this viewpoint is that many of the ideas outlined in these works are complicated, vague, or incomplete. They do not make up a true evaluation of relevant ethical issues.

A third approach questions the conceptual or the theoretical set-up of Sartrean ethics. This understanding comes from the heresy that Sartre's posthumous works lack a theoretical foundation. I refer to this examination as "the theoretical argument."

The disputed point is that Sartre's posthumously released materials lack a clear theoretical foundation. The position that has been gathered from this approach projects the claims which are regularly expressed about Sartre posthumously released writings. According to this misguided approach, Sartre's works on ethics are abstract, disjointed, and rudimentary.

These works are incomplete. There is no doubt about that reality. It could be said that these works are under similar conditions, not because Sartre could not conceptualize his views compellingly. Rather, Sartre made a deliberate choice to keep them in these formats.

A few works, including scholarly and non-scholarly publications, are unambiguously opposed to the chance that Sartre could ever be considered a canonized writer in the ethical discipline. The publication argument is often evoked to disprove the nature of Sartrean ethics. Critics often use this popular view to dismiss Sartre's importance in philosophy as well.

Here is an important actually; Sartre was aware of his works. He was doubtless aware of the limits of his arguments. He admitted that his examinations of ethical issues were still embryonic.

Sartre admitted that his works were underdeveloped. Sartre accepted that some ideas he outlined about ethics were still under construction. This suggests that Sartre only abandoned his works on ethics as a deliberate strategy to focus on other literary ventures.

Sartre hinted that he intended to return to his ethical writings at the proper time.[4] The argument of "incompleteness" does little to lessen Sartre's status as a moral philosopher. Making such claims should not have the inclination to alter Sartre's works in ethical discipline.

ARGUING IN SARTRE'S FAVOR

Is it prudent to author a book about Jean-Paul Sartre? Is it safe to address the disapproval that is echoed against him? Would a person require any guidance to answer these questions? A likely answer would be no.

Many people would swear that Sartre was not a moral philosopher. Not every criticism is an ill intent of Sartre. Some observers genuinely believe that the Sartrean approach ethics is not that coherent. I do not argue for the opposite. As inferred earlier, Sartrean ethics is not all that it could be, even if Sartre devoted a portion of his time to it.

---

[4] To learn more about this idea, see (Johnson 2016)

There are those critics who seem hell bent on disproving Sartre, no matter what. Here is where my defense of Jean-Paul Sartre is important. The prevailing misconception is that Sartre did little in the ethical domain. To support this view, critics often point out that not only Sartre published fewer items on ethics, but these items are also inconclusive. This is patently false.

The popular mindset is that Sartre is ineligible for the title of a moral philosopher. Many observers have contended that ethics had not been Sartre's strongest suit. There is truth in the earlier perspective. That is not all. There is more to the issues than debating the extent of Sartre's relevance in the ethical domain.

Sartre did not contribute enormously to the ethical genre. Critics often overlooked other important reasons. They undermine the evidence that could solidify the notion that Sartre played a prominent role in the field. In effect, they disallowed the likelihood of a Sartrean role in ethics in every way imaginable.

Theoretical beliefs about the ethical works that Sartre produced could be difficult to decipher. Yes, the ideas he explained in his writings could be complicated. The notion that any insight Sartre might have had in this discipline must be insignificant based solely on the works he produced is in error.

Sartre had developed a true ethic in his philosophy. Because of this understanding, my position is obvious. Sartre deserves to be recognized as a moral philosopher.

Based on the earlier logic, arguing in favor of the Sartrean ethical model is not such a futile intellectual effort on my part. After making the earlier case, let me further note that I recognize that I lack the intellectual courage necessary to defend Sartrean ethics. That does not mean that trying to achieve this goal is a chimerical project.

Most observers, whether they have the ability in philosophy, often feel that it is okay for them to criticize Sartre willy-nilly. Why should I not defend this great thinker in the same manner that others criticize him, despite my limited intellectual bravery to do so adequately? This is a legitimate question to ask, considering the literary atmosphere about Sartre.

Another question is why critics abound against Sartre. Why do observers deny the Sartrean moral thoughts? One may not hold the needed certainty about how to answer these questions without echoing my bias into the debate.

What is certain is the criticisms, which weaken the Sartrean literary valor, are unmerited. They are, to say the least, shortsighted. Sartre is not given the credit for his works in the ethical discipline. It is important to examine the nature of existing criticisms relentlessly. This is what I have done in two of my publications. Please refer to the text titled *Sartrean Ethics and Jean-Paul Sartre and Morality* to learn more.

EPISTEMOLOGICAL RELEVANCE

Sifting through Sartre's ethical thoughts can be a daunting task for most. Claiming to be the exception would be a mischaracterization. I always thought I needed to gain more information about the man and his philosophy. I assumed that it might be necessary to catalog the principles of the ideas that Sartre sought to advance in his works before defending them.

I must confess that I was perplexed about my ability to evaluate the confines of Sartrean ethics. I never considered Sartre's ethical thoughts separate from his philosophical brand.

I never thought of ethics as a standalone field that deserves intellectual scrutiny.

As I delved into the literature, my understanding of the issues broadened. My confidence to complete a relevant piece of literature grew exponentially. That could explain my urge to defend Sartre.

As a fan of Sartre's works, the more I investigated his principles, the more I realized that Sartre's thoughts are common in his works. Such ideas are omnipresent throughout his major works. It is central to stress the ethical implications of these works to their fullest.

When I read books, blog posts, or scholarly articles about Sartre, even when I examine strictures that question Sartre's method of deciphering ethics, I often feel the need to respond. The urge to disagree with these arguments was futile. Over time, I realized my epistemological limits in the field. I agree to follow the debate. This book is a genuine effort to change that outlook.

My position is that Sartre was a philosopher of human conditions. This view is because the Sartrean method of human ontology is intertwined with ethics. Sartre did not need to explore ethics separately from human ontology.

Most observers disagree on the materiality of Sartre's moral thoughts. Denying his role in human morality or challenging his contribution to philosophy (as a whole) is wrong. I echoed this view clearly in the present context.

SECTION 5

Proving My Relevance in the Debate

11. ARGUMENTATIVE RELEVANCE

Now that I have pointed a few argumentative flaws in the conversation against Jean-Paul Sartre, you might still be perplexed about the reason compiling a book defending Sartre was necessary. Let me echo from the outset that it is important to explain why the debate over the role Sartre played on moral philosophy. There is a need to defend anyone who works are lambasted because those who refute those works are blinded by the facts or they have fallen prey to an ideological illness, which prevents them from being impartial in their approach to ideas that undermine their own views.

Despite the previous justifications for fending Jean-Paul Sartre, you might still wonder what led me to compile this work. Well, this pamphlet came about for several reasons. Outlining all of them seemed unnecessary. I must mention my liking for literature, modern philosophy.[1]

Another important reason to point out is the pursuit of academic excellence. After drafting several essays about Jean-Paul Sartre and his major philosophical ideas, I compiled a

---

[1]. My academic interest is centered on French literature. French is my native language. Both my elementary and secondary education is based on the French schooling system.

summary of Sartrean ethics. It was hard to pass up the opportunity to turn the document into a textbook.

One thing led to another. As the word counts compounded, I realized that one treatise might not be enough to carry the message I wanted to share about Sartre. It might be important to defend this great thinker in human literature.

Splitting my original work into several manuscripts was a practical choice. Upholding the same argument was important. Sartre has undeniable literary relevance in ethics. This text was compiled under a similar prism.

This publication was born of the want to bring a reflective tool into the discussion about the extent of Sartrean philosophy. This document could be considered a preparatory work which should help the reader become familiar with my major points of strife in the literature. The goal is to allow the reader to understand the extent of Sartrean philosophy as a whole, as well as the Sartrean approach to human morality.

Despite the arguments I outline in my works, I am still obsessed with preserving the sanctity of the Sartrean legacy in ethics. Put another way, I want to highlight Sartre's works on ethics. The goal is to defend the extent of Sartrean ethics symbolized such a defense is possible.

OUTLINING MY GOALS

This text was developed to offer the reader a reasonable assessment of existing issues in the debate. It stimulated interest in the writings Sartre compiled on several topics. The hope is to stimulate the reader's curiosity about Sartre's *bona fide* literary valor. That is the reason the emphasis here is on the Sartrean contribution to human literature, moral philosophy.

An alternative goal is to infuse a balanced view into the current literary conversation. The debate is too slanted against

Sartre. Another aim of this work was to create a tool that would help the average reader make sense of the current debate. That could help appease the fervor against Sartre.

This work came about for various reasons. It stemmed from the expectation that it would offer valuable information to scholars and casual readers alike. The goal is to tell those unfamiliar with Sartre about his relevance in ethics. The views expressed in this manual come from several sources.

My works about Sartre reference academic and other types of sources. References include popular texts or books, peer-reviewed articles, magazines, websites, blogs, and newspapers, just to name a few. Thus, the views echoed in this case are not based on subjective opinions in a genuine sense of the term.

The goal is to promote an even plain field to support those who believe that Sartre has a well-deserved place in the ethical discipline. Through the writings featured, readers may grapple with Sartre's examination of human morality as objectively as possible. This collection could become a reference tool.

CONTRIBUTION TO THE LITERATURE

Being actively involved in this project was intellectually rewarding. I gained useful insights from the writing of this volume. The same viewpoint holds for the other works that I have compiled on Sartre. A few intellectual benefits are worthy of mention. Completing this text was a delight. I also learned a lot from this experience both personally and academically.

Gathering my ideas in a coherent format was intellectually grueling. English is not my native tongue. Thus, completing this work was an opportunity to fine-tune my writings. This method helped in research techniques and analytical skills.[2]

Conquering my want to produce reading materials that would be worthy of your time and intellectual curiosity was impossible. Another problem is that finding a satisfactory way to feature Sartre under an impartial light was hard. defending Sartre with the most objective lens was equally challenging.

The project consumed most of my free time. After careful considerations, I settled on the current versions. They include Sartrean Ethics and Jean-Paul Sartre and morality.

When researching the topic, I exhausted my limits. I was lost in my determination to find the aim views about Sartre. It took me a while to accept the idea the literature was against Sartre. I found it hard to find publications that would express a neutral view of Sartrean ethics.

Examining the extent of Sartrean philosophy was an opportunity to strengthen my understanding of the "Existentialist" model. I learned a lot about the issue that usually plague the conversation. Finding novel criticisms was impossible. Most of the ideas echoed in the literature are repetitive and disjointed. I navigated the literature.

This work was inspired by several pedagogical concerns. It was necessary to produce a softback that would capture the essence of Sartrean ethics. I wanted to compile a book that would be informative and intellectually entertaining. It became urgent to gather ideas that would engage readers who might be unfamiliar with the topic but would also incite intellectual curiosity among Sartrean scholars or other experts.

---

[2]. My skills have expanded two-fold. After completing so many drafts, I am pleased with the current version. I feel confident that the reader will agree with that assessment. I hope to improve the quality of this work in future editions.

ACADEMIC VALUE OF THIS BOOK

This work instilled academic excellence. Academic relevance influenced my efforts. These concerns led me to this work. Sartre is not treated right in the literature. I wanted to defend him to the extent I could do so coherently.

To defend Sartre, it was necessary to reference other works, which are part of the literature. It was necessary to set up my arguments so they could reflect the current literary conversation. It might be hard to convince others that Sartre has relevance in ethics. That is not a reason not to try.

There is not much room for any appreciation of the Sartrean ethical ideal. The literature is filled with criticisms and claims against Sartre. There is a want to undermine the Sartre's well-earned legacy. It became essential to mitigate this reality.

Some views echoed in the literature can be appalling. Sartre is often portrayed as a misguided thinker. Here, the belief is that Sartre himself is often lost in the ideas that he invokes to enlighten others. Of course, this is ludicrous.

There is not much love for Sartre in the debate. There is a not a unique way to change that dynamic. The extent to which this work did the unintended possibility stays unclear.

The views presented in this collection might help tilt the debate in Sartre's favor. Not all observations on Sartrean ethics are negative. The text titled Sartrean Ethics explains as convincingly as possible that many scholars are fond of the Sartrean approach to moral philosophy.[3]

Although Sartre is known as a philosopher, his views about ethics are contested. One could make the case that Sartrean ethics is of a different range. Explain this

---

[3] To learn more about this idea, see (Johnson 2016)

understanding as clearly as possible in my work made up the foundation of the analysis of this edition.

In defending Sartre, it was critical to highlight his ethics. It was principal to do so with a positive lens. Drawing supports for my arguments was only possible by referencing the works by several scholars who have echoed a more positive outlook toward Sartre. It was also fitting to focus on the works published by scholars in one part of the literature.[4]

During the 1990s, several scholars echoed some positive features of Sartre. Although their works have been acclaimed in the literature, the ideas they suggested are not always considered. The positions proposed by these scholars have not been rebuffed or challenged. Disagreements persist in the debate. What might explain this persistence is unclear. That does not mean that we could not guess.

In my other publications on the subject, the views expressed in the previously mentioned works serve as a guide to understand the debate and to craft relevant responses to some of the most verbose statements. These ideas became a reference point to support the positions that Sartre was indeed a moral philosopher. Accepting that the Sartrean approach to ethics is not perfect would not be a misnomer.

What is irrefutable is the literature is laden with claims that look to rebuke Sartre. The position resounded by previously noted scholars is that Sartrean ethics are intellectually relevant. They believe that Sartre's ethics are not without flaws. It was central to underline that sentiment in the most succinct, but also logically, throughout this anthology.

---

[4] To learn more about this idea, see text titled Sartrean Ethics. See (Johnson 2016, 105–14).

12. Pedagogical Concerns

Several pedagogical concerns led me to complete this work. They are relevant; they show the foundation of this literary effort. A proper classification for them would be "excellent." Thus, they are worth mentioning.

These concerns have informed my interest in the topic two-fold. They are crystallized in four ways: (1) inciting a real debate; (2) examining commentaries; (3) encouraging further inquiries; and (4) starting a sincere pleading on Sartre's behalf. Let us explore these concerns in depth.

Analyzing Sartrean ethics was to be distinctly objective. Bringing about a balanced debate about Sartre is not a simple task. Sartre was a polarized figure. It was vital to stress that criticisms against the reach of Sartrean ethics are disjointed; they are also contradictory.

Despite popular condemnations, Sartre's style to examine ethics is undeniably relevant. It might be difficult to defend the Sartrean method to ethics beyond doubt. Granted, this ethical model is not without flaws.

It might be difficult to claim the Sartrean slant to ethics is in an unblemished state. Presenting a succinct view of the true extent of the Sartrean examination of ethical cases is still an elusive project. Keep these limits in mind as you explore my other works on the subject.

There might be a genuine need to study the nature of Sartrean ethics. Such inquiries must first consider the nature of the works that Sartre produced. They should not only rely on these works. There is a shortfall of productive criticisms about Sartre. His approach to ethics is rebuffed in the literature with no alternative considerations. One could not be certain as to the reason the Sartrean slant on ethics is so obscure; if not, I would refer to is as one-sided.

My primary aim in defending Sartre does not center on challenging disapproval viewpoints against the man or against his philosophy altogether. The disagreements with Sartre seem fair, well founded and to the point. Few critics recognize that Sartre was trying to be in several places at once. Assessment of the works Sartre produced must be based on their quality and not on their content.

There is a longing for a better examination of Sartrean ethics. Sometimes criticisms seem too intrusive, too devaluing, and dismissive. Such a condemnation, as the goal was to point out here, rarely consider the nature of Sartre's intellectual worth. There is a need for intellectual conviviality and academic civility in the debate.

This work was not intended to call out every misguided attack against Sartre. It must be noted that even though the literature is laden with commentaries and other forms of analysis, often by famous philosophers (in this case, Richard Bernstein) and well-known scholars (for example, David Pellauer), the gist of the debate is often filled (or polluted) by speculations and assumptions about Sartre. The hope was to change the current story, which is heading, increasingly, toward an aggressive state against a deceased thinker.[1] It is important to have a productive method to examine the Sartrean model.

A NEED FOR PRODUCTIVE CRITICISMS

There is a lack of positive criticism in the literature against Sartre. There is a lack of views that are not just destructive but also informative. Intellectual grievances that bridge existing gaps in Sartrean writings would be more impressive as opposed to a mere complaint, which effects might be solely to point out those gaps and to offer no alternatives.

A better use of our time might be to promote a productive critique of the Sartrean ethical model. The text informed the reader. The goal is to guide the reader about the argument against Sartre. Another goal, although implicitly stated, is to reinforce positive views about Sartre and his works.

A subtler goal is to encourage further inquiries about the views often echoed against Sartre. Views that are often echoed against Sartre in the most long-winded manner deserve more exposure. Many of such views rebuff the works Sartre produced about ethics exclusive of reprieve and short of substance.

Arguments indexed by prominent scholars often want a thorough examination. However, such a concise scrutiny is often deficient. This work looked to fill that gap, though it sought to do so summarily.

This is a reference manual. The goal is to describe false ideas about Sartre. It explores arbitrary claims against Sartre's works.

---

[1]. I am referring to Jean-Paul Sartre.

This volume stimulated sensible reflections on Sartrean ethics. Sartre outlined a clear theoretical foundation in his works, which would be apt for his writing about ethics. Sartre's method for exploring ethics is present in his works, some of which were published posthumously. They include his acclaimed works on human ontology.

This primer offers a response to those who disagree that Sartre is a moral philosopher. It supports those who recognize the possibility that Sartre played a role in ethics, though a small contribution. In the same way, the paperbound came about to offer a counterargument against those who challenge the Sartrean approach to moral philosophy.

SUMMARY OF MAJOR ARGUMENTS

After reviewing countless works by Sartre on ethics, his exquisite method overwhelmed my literary senses. A sense of urgency became obvious to me. The want to defend Sartre expresses that experience. This led me to review the ideas that Sartre proposed in his works. That experience also led me to realize that many of the works Sartre produced were (often) undervalued. May it please be carping critics, *N'en déplaise aux critiqueurs*—no offense to critics, Sartre deserves recognition as an important thinker in ethics.

The earlier viewpoint emanates from the understanding that Sartrean ethics is not, from within, a separate entity in Sartrean philosophy. This approach to ethics does not require a separate theoretical basis. Critics levy inequitable charges against Sartre, notably when they recognize that the man earned a well-deserved relevance in other philosophical realms. It was necessary to argue for a better appreciation of the role that Sartre undeniably played in the ethical domain as plainly as possible.

It is important to encourage those who may be curious about the reach of Sartre's moral thoughts not to limit themselves to comments that appear too critical, too one-sided, or even too arbitrary. It was material to echo that Sartre was a relevant thinker in many respects, specifically in ethics. Upholding this view, I must concede—despite the current debate—might be far more complex than previously thought.

A Sartrean philosophical bearing extends beyond existentialism. His works on ethics are suitable for the ethical discipline. Such works, as echoed in this context, deserve a better intellectual treatment. This is so contrary to the way these works are examined, there is an absence of a nicer method to discussing the crux of Sartrean ethics.

Sartre deserves more consideration. His writings on ethics are undervalued. Despite many claims, his works are not in such a mediocre state. Sartre deserves better than that, has argued in this work.

An important goal deeply proven in this work is to highlight Sartre's intellectual efforts in philosophy. There ought to be a re-evaluation of Sartre as a writer, a thinker, a philosopher, and as a moralist. It is necessary to explore the role Sartre played in ethics. That assessment must also be comprehensive.

A HOLISTIC APPROACH

The arguments outlined throughout this text are straightforward. The goal was to propose a comprehensive approach to the debate, which would make it possible to perform the tasks listed at the outset of the manuscript. As you discover my philosophical works, you might face similar views or the same recommendations. Such viewpoints are inserted into the many issues debated in this manuscript. Similar observations can be clear in my other works on the subject.

Critiquing the literary conversation is not personal, though it might be difficult to deny my own idiosyncrasies. It applied to explore the extent of Sartrean ethics. It became clear since the beginning of this project that doing so might not be simple.

The pervious view being foreshadowed, it might be noteworthy that my positions had not been provocative, vindictive, or even disrespectful to those who hold dissenting viewpoints toward Sartre. Despite this reality, one could not overlook the arguments, which are shortsighted. It might be impossible to ignore claims, which came across as being misguided in their assessment of Sartre's works, specifically when considering the Sartrean slant to ethics. It is principally important not to jump on the anti-Sartre bandwagon.

It was fundamental to call out those who appear intransigent in their examination of Sartrean ethics. Overlooking their intellectual bad faith in this case was inconceivable. The preeminence of this work was to call these people out in their inaccurate criticisms; at least, it was pressing to at least try to do so here.

Having explained why I considered defending the Sartrean legacy as cardinal, I hope that you found my explanations interesting enough. Anyway, it might not be exaggerated to encourage you (that is, the reader) to learn more about Sartre. There are enough materials to learn about the true nature of Jean-Paul Sartre. There is much information to help you discover the man and his most intriguing works. If you are so inclined, you may learn more about my philosophy, particularly as it depicts human ontology.

If you would like to learn more about Sartre, the debate, or even my other works on the subject, you may see the books titled Sartrean Ethics and Jean-Paul Sartre and Morality. These works offer a deeper understanding of the debate. They outline the role Sartre played in present-day literature.

Other than referring to my other publications in the philosophical domain, you might indulge in more works produced by Jean-Paul Sartre. Depending on your intellectual leaning, you might find the need to defend Sartre as well. To echo a popular French saying, à bon entendeur, salut. Otherwise, a word to the wise is enough.

CONCLUSION

O bservers might assume that the text has no academic value. Some might even contend that this work only shows my bias about the extent of Sartrean ethics. It does not prove that ethics. Defending the Sartrean legacy is more complex than this work could explain.

As far as the relevance of this work, let me point out that there is enough reason to share my apprehension about the course of the conversation about Sartre's works. While it may seem obvious to some observers, Sartre's works are virulently despised in the literature. One could not find works that load the man and his literary competence. Compiling a text that solidifies Sartre as both a writer and a moral philosopher is important.

It might be worth pointing out that looking to challenge those who often see no intellectual use for Sartrean ethics was not the intent. Instead, the goal was to present another side of the debate. Accomplishing this aim was supreme in the present context.

It may be plain to see that one could not defend Sartre without raising questions about those who often rebuke him. However, it was far from a stated goal to lessen, at least as vocally as possible, those who rebuke Sartre on the intellectual plane field. It was not a primary goal to belittle their examination of Sartre's moral thoughts, considering that Sartre's works on moral philosophy are not perfect. Approaching the issues from a different organ was the ideal, if not the urgency, which guided this project.

Whether implicitly or else, most people know that Jean-Paul Sartre is immortal, at least intellectually. His thoughts left a permanent mark on human literature. His works are of incommensurable value. To that effect, Sartre lives on chiefly through his ideas, his thoughts, and his works about human ontology, which are intertwined with his positions about human morality. It was important to point that out in this writing.

Before ending this conversation, it is worth outlining that the views echoed here are far from perfect. They did not emanate from a connoisseur of Sartrean ethics, which I hope I did not suggest in writing this compendium. Claiming to be a Sartrean scholar, and that, by any stretch of the imagination, would be dangerously pompous on my part. I tried not to suggest such a presumption here.

Being exposed to the existentialist model was not a precondition to complete this text. Being an expert in Sartrean philosophy is not a requirement to defend Jean-Paul Sartre. However, being fascinated by Sartre's slant on phenomenology played a critical role in helping me make up a position, I hope, sounded intellectually intriguing or even argumentatively coherent. These were the original goals in compiling this work.

To avoid any doubt in your understanding of my intent here, let me point out that the analysis suggested in these pages was not set up as an authoritative voice on Sartrean ethics. Not that these examinations could not enlighten you (that is, the reader) about the crux of that ethics. A Sartrean mode of examining ethics is more complicated than might be obvious.

Thus, it was necessary to make the debate more bearable, more malleable, and even it bit intellectually appealing to the average reader.

Let me note that the earlier confession is neither a ploy nor a way to avoid criticism for compiling this text in its current format. Questioning the quality of this work or even debating the need for the views echoed here would be welcome. Remember the earlier admission does not excuse any errors in this work, be they analytical or factual.

It is indisputable that the Sartrean legacy is under attack. This work defended that heritage. Keep in mind that this compilation is not the product of an empirical study. Thus, the views expressed in the book are biased. They came from my valuation of the literature.

In conclusion, Jean-Paul Sartre lives on. The man is immortalized through his works, even though the literature may not be gracious toward Sartre himself and his major accomplishments. It was important to defend this great thinker. It was essential to be as succinct as possible in my evaluation of the current debate.

Despite the efforts taken to present a sound analysis of the Sartrean model, this work is not flawless. As they say, l'erreur est du domaine de l'homme; the error is human. Therefore, presenting this work as a faultless depiction of the debate about Sartrean ethics would be dishonest on my part.

The analysis outlined throughout the book reflects my judgment of the views expressed in the debate. The focus was on the Sartrean approach to ethics. The book explored issues often noted in books, magazines, and other materials. The goal was to favor an honest review of Sartre's works both while alive and posthumously. The success of this publication will be based on how you (that is, the reader) make consider it worthy in the debate about Jean-Paul Sartre and his philosophical brand.

REFERENCES

Anderson, Thomas C. 2002a. "Jean-Paul Sartre: From an Existentialist to a Realistic Ethics." In *Phenomenological Approaches to Moral Philosophy: A Handbook*, edited by John J. Drummond and Lester Embree, 367–89. Contributions to Phenomenology. Dordrecht: Springer Netherlands. https://doi.org/10.1007/978-94-015-9924-5_19.

———. 2002b. "Beyond Sartre's Ethics of Authenticity." *Journal of the British Society for Phenomenology* 33 (2): 138–54. https://doi.org/10.1080/00071773.2002.11007376.

Aronson, Ronald, and Adrian Van Den Hoven, eds. 1991. *Sartre Alive*. Detroit: Wayne State University Press.

Arthur, Paige. 2007. "Remembering Sartre." *Theory and Society* 36 (3): 231–43. https://doi.org/10.1007/s11186-007-9034-0.

Bernstein, Richard J. 2011. *Praxis and Action: Contemporary Philosophies of Human Activity*. University of Pennsylvania Press.

Birchall, Ian H. 2004. *Sartre Against Stalinism*. Berghahn Books.

CCM Benchmark. 2022. "Le Génie n'a Qu'un Siècle, Après Quoi, Il Faut Qu'il Dégénère." 2022. http://www.linternaute.com/citation/13020/le-genie-n-a-qu-un-siecle--apres-quoi--il-faut-qu-il---voltaire/.

Cline, Austin. 2019. "Karl Marx on Religion as the Opium of the People." Learn Religions. January 7, 2019. https://www.learnreligions.com/karl-marx-on-religion-251019.

Cooper, David. 1964. "Sartre on Genet." *New Left Review*, no. I/25 (June): 69–73.

Crittenden, Paul. 1998. "The Singular Universal in Jean-Paul Sartre." *Literature & Aesthetics* 8: 29–42.

Emerick, Rex. 1999. "Sartre's Theory of Emotions: A Reply to His Critics." *Sartre Studies International* 5 (2): 75–91. https://doi.org/10.3167/135715599782368597.

Flynn, Thomas R. 1986. *Sartre and Marxist Existentialism: The Test Case of Collective Responsibility*. University of Chicago Press.

———. 2000. "Times Squared: Historical Time in Sartre and Foucault." In *The Many Faces of Time*, edited by John B. Brough and Lester Embree, 203–22. Contributions to Phenomenology. Dordrecht: Springer Netherlands. https://doi.org/10.1007/978-94-015-9411-0_11.

———. 2005. "Sartre at One Hundred: A Man of the Nineteenth Century Addressing the Twenty-First?" *Sartre Studies International* 11 (1): 1–14. https://doi.org/10.3167/135715505780282560.

Fraser, Mariam. 1999. *Identity Without Selfhood: Simone de Beauvoir and Bisexuality*. Cambridge University Press.

Gothlin, Eva. 1999. "Simone de Beauvoir's Notions of Appeal, Desire, and Ambiguity and Their Relationship to Jean-Paul Sartre's Notions of Appeal and Desire." *Hypatia* 14 (4): 83–95. https://doi.org/10.1111/j.1527-2001.1999.tb01254.x.

Hoven, Adrian Van den, and Andrew N. Leak. 2005. *Sartre Today: A Centenary Celebration*. Berghahn Books.

Johnson, Ben Wood. 2016. *Sartrean Ethics: A Defense of Jean-Paul Sartre As A Moral Philosopher*. Eduka Solutions.

———. 2017. *Jean-Paul Sartre and Morality: A Legacy Under Attack*. 1 edition. Eduka Solutions.

LaCapra, Dominick. 2019. *A Preface to Sartre*. Cornell University Press.

Ledgerwood, Mikle D. 1990. "Howells, Christina. Sartre: The Necessity of Freedom. Cambridge, UK: Cambridge University Press, 1988." *The Canadian Modern Language Review* 46 (4): 765–67. https://doi.org/10.3138/cmlr.46.4.765.

Levin, David Michael. 1968. "On Lévi-Strauss and
    Existentialism." *The American Scholar* 38 (1): 69–82.
Levi-strauss, Claude. 1966. *The Savage Mind*. University of
    Chicago Press.
Linsenbard, Gail Evelyn. 2000. *An Investigation of Jean-Paul Sartre's
    Posthumously Published Notebooks for an Ethics*. Edwin
    Mellen Press.
Lloyd, Rosemary, and Jean Fornasiero. 2014. *Magnificent
    Obsessions: Honouring the Lives of Hazel Rowley*. Cambridge
    Scholars Publishing.
Martinot, Steve. 1999. "The Site of Postmodernity in Sartre."
    Sartre Studies International 5 (2): 45–60.
    https://doi.org/10.3167/135715599782368614.
Marx, Karl. 2001. *Marxism, Socialism and Religion*. Resistance
    Books.
Mcdonnell, Hugh. 2020. "Jean-Paul Sartre the European."
    Modern Intellectual History 17 (1): 147–77.
    https://doi.org/10.1017/S1479244318000148.
McEwen, Todd, and Lucy Ellmann. 2006. "Damp Squibs." *The
    Guardian*, January 14, 2006, sec. Books.
    http://www.theguardian.com/books/2006/jan/14/hig
    hereducation.biography.
Meszaros, Istvan. 2012. *The Work of Sartre*. New York: Monthly
    Review Press.
Murphy, Julien S. 1999. *Feminist Interpretations of Jean-Paul Sartre*.
    Penn State Press.
Poellner, Peter. 2016. "Action, Value, and Autonomy: A Quasi-
    Sartrean View." In *Comparing Kant and Sartre*, edited by
    Sorin Baiasu, 132–57. London: Palgrave Macmillan UK.
    https://doi.org/10.1057/9781137454539_7.
Raynova, Yvanka B. 2002. "Jean-Paul Sartre, a Profound
    Revision of Husserlian Phenomenology." In
    *Phenomenology World-Wide: Foundations — Expanding
    Dynamics — Life-Engagements. A Guide for Research and
    Study*, edited by A. Ales Bello, M. Antonelli, G.
    Backhaus, O. Balaban, G. Baptist, J. Bengtsson, J.
    Benoist, et al., 323–35. Analecta Husserliana.
    Dordrecht: Springer Netherlands.
    https://doi.org/10.1007/978-94-007-0473-2_34.

Sartre, Jean-Paul. 2001. *Colonialism and Neocolonialism*. London: Routledge. https://doi.org/10.4324/9780203991848.

————. 2002. *Jean-Paul Sartre: Basic Writings*. Edited by Stephen Priest. 0 ed. Routledge. https://doi.org/10.4324/9780203129647.

Sartre, Jean-Paul, and Sarah Richmond. 2022. *Being and Nothingness: An Essay in Phenomenological Ontology*. London: Routledge. https://doi.org/10.4324/9780429434013.

Suhl, Benjamin. 1999. *Jean-Paul Sartre: The Philosopher as a Literary Critic*. iUniverse.

Warnock, Mary. 1966. Review of *Review of The Marxism of Jean-Paul Sartre*, by Wilfred Desan. *The Journal of Philosophy* 63 (23): 757–61. https://doi.org/10.2307/2024278.

Williams, Dan. 2015. "Sartre's Theory of Imagination and The Seventh Seal." In *Klein, Sartre and Imagination in the Films of Ingmar Bergman*, edited by Dan Williams, 67–95. London: Palgrave Macmillan UK. https://doi.org/10.1057/9781137471987_3.

Wreszin, Michael. 1961. "Jean-Paul Sartre: Philosopher as Dramatist." *Tulane Drama Review* 5 (3): 34–57. https://doi.org/10.2307/1124661.

INDEX

This index includes some of the most frequent words and terms used in this document. Note that the eBook version of this manuscript does not include an index segment.

ABOUT THE AUTHOR

BEN WOOD JOHNSON, PH.D.
Dr. Johnson is a philosopher, author, and educator. He is a multidisciplinary scholar. He teaches criminal justice at Penn State University, Harrisburg. Dr. Johnson writes about philosophy, legal theory, public and foreign policy, education (Leadership), politics, ethics, race, and crime.

Dr. Johnson is a Penn State graduate. He holds a Doctorate in Educational Administration/Leadership, a Master's degree in Political Science (Villanova University), a Master's degree in Public Administration, and a Bachelor's degree in Criminal Justice.

Dr. Johnson is a retired police officer. He attended John Jay College of Criminal Justice. Dr. Johnson is fluent in many languages, including, but not limited to, English, French, Spanish, Portuguese, and Italian. He enjoys reading, poetry, painting, and music.

You may contact Dr. Johnson in the address below.

Electronic Address:

E-mail: benwoodpost@gmail.com

Other Info:

You may find Dr. Johnson on the following media platforms.

Twitter handle is @benwoodpost

Facebook @benwoodpost

Blogs: www.benwoodpost.com

Official website: www.benwoodjohnson.com

Other Publications:

Other works by Dr. Johnson include:

- Racism: What is it?
- Sartrean Ethics: A Defense of Jean-Paul Sartre as a Moral Philosopher
- Jean-Paul Sartre and Morality: A Legacy Under Attack
- Forced Out of Vietnam: A Policy Analysis of the Fall of Saigon
- Natural Law: Morality and Obedience
- Cogito Ergo Philosophus
- Citizen Obedience: The Nature of Legal Obligation
- Le Racisme et le Socialisme: La Discrimination Raciale dans un Milieu Capitaliste
- International Law: The Rise of Russia as a Global Threat
- Être Noir: Quel Malheur!
- L'homme et le Racisme: Être Responsable de vos Actions et Omissions
- Pennsylvania Inspired Leadership: A Roadmap for American Educators
- Adult Education in America: A Policy Assessment of Adult Learning
- Striving to Survive: The Human Migration Story.

www.ingramcontent.com/pod-product-compliance
Lightning Source LLC
Chambersburg PA
CBHW031626040426
42452CB00007B/704